The Burden of the Past

The Burden of the Past and the English Poet

W. Jackson Bate

The Belknap Press of
Harvard University Press
Cambridge, Massachusetts
1970

Distributed in Great Britain by Oxford University Press, London

Illustration (p. i): H. Fuseli, "The Artist Moved by the Grandeur of Ancient Ruins," 1778–79. Kunsthaus Zürich.

Library of Congress Catalog Card Number 70–102666
SBN 674–08586–8

Printed in the United States of America

To David Perkins

Preface

This book consists of the Alexander Lectures given at the University of Toronto in November 1969.

The broader concern is what seems to me the principal dilemma facing the artist generally from the Renaissance to the present day. With that concern in mind, these lectures focus on the first major example of this dilemma: the position of the English poet between the English Renaissance – the epoch of Shakespeare and Milton – and the Victorians and near-moderns (1660 to 1830). For a number of reasons, some of them discussed in this book, the full weight on the modern artist of what I have called "the burden of the past" pressed first upon the poet; and it was in England especially that the problem became dramatized, at the same time inciting three generations of brilliant discussion of the artist's relation to the past.

The pivotal period is the eighteenth century. It is this period that made the turn from Renaissance to modern. In the process it discovered the costs as well as the gains of a self-consciousness unparalleled in degree at any time before. If there was trauma, there was also honesty: honesty both to fact and to essential ideal. This is what is most relevant – perhaps most reassuring – about the eighteenth century to us now as we look for companionship or help in our own attempt to clear the head and get closer to essentials.

The discussion of any particular theme is by definition exclusive. I have felt this personally, as I here focus solely on a subject treated in different contexts in other books, including biographical studies of Johnson, Coleridge, and Keats. (In the case of Coleridge and Keats especially, a major interest was the challenge and embarrassment of past achievement to the modern creative mind in the arts.) A wealth of other considerations (historical, biographical, critical) are naturally relevant at every point and in an ampler study of these two centuries would be given – and have in the past often been given — consideration. I concentrate on this one issue because I feel it has been lost sight of for a variety of reasons. One is the post-romantic historicism that too mechanically assumes that we are weather vanes before the wind of the *Zeitgeist* — passive creatures of a phenomenon described as "the historical changes in sensibility."

What permits the single-mindedness of this discussion — the fact that it consists of four lectures on just one theme — may also excuse a certain amount of repetition: the restating of the theme at the start of each lecture and at various points within them. I should also say that if there seems a tone of fatalistic determinism as I try to describe a trauma and a courageous if painful effort toward self-clarification and regrounding, I myself have no feeling of the inevitable decline of the arts. My personal belief, for whatever it is worth, could be summarized by Johnson's remark about the influence of weather on the imagination of poets who feel they can work only at certain times: When such an idea "has possession of the head," it "produces the inability which it supposes." This is perhaps putting it too abruptly. But I believe that if man is not completely a free agent, he is at least freer than he often thinks he is.

I should add a final note. These lectures, aside from their more general theme, were conceived in a spirit of protest against the continued stubbornness, in our universities, of professional compartmentalization between what is reductively or simple-mindedly considered the "eighteenth century" and the "Romantic," with a portcullis dropping at 1798 or some approximate date. For over a generation many gifted minds have tried to break down this fictitious wall of ours between the "eighteenth century" and the children it educated. But the stock tendency is still to regard the eighteenth century as mainly the product of men born and educated in the seventeenth. I myself would say that what a century creates, and the youth that it brings to maturity, are quite as relevant to our understanding of the period, if not more so. The essence of the eighteenth century is the creation of the "Romantic" and, in a variety of ways, the modern.

I express thanks to the University of Toronto for their invitation to give these lectures; to the Director of the Johns Hopkins University Press for permission to reprint part of a lecture with a similar title (published in *Aspects of the Eighteenth Century*, ed. Earl Wasserman, 1965); to the Kunsthaus Zürich for permission to reproduce the drawing by Henry Fuseli, "The Artist Moved by the Grandeur of Ancient Ruins," and for their courtesy in providing a photograph of it; to Professor Walter Kaiser of Harvard, who has helped me in many ways and who first told me of the Fuseli drawing; and to Judith Plotz, now completing a comprehensive study of the concept of decline in the arts from 1660 through the Romantics. Friends and colleagues elsewhere will note my use of ideas of their own: I think particularly of Professors Earl Wasserman, Northrop Frye, Harold Bloom, and Geoffrey Tillotson.

I am especially indebted to three colleagues at Harvard – Professors Douglas Bush, Harry Levin, and David Perkins – with whom I have long discussed this subject and others related to it. While warmly sympathizing with my attempt to present it briefly in this form, they have also, time and again, helped to clear my mind – as Sir Joshua Reynolds said in his tribute to Johnson – of "a great deal of rubbish." In inscribing this book to Professor Perkins, I also express my gratitude for the ways in which he has at once challenged and encouraged me over the years to interpret the eighteenth century and the Romantics generally in the light of the more modern experience of the arts, as he had more particularly done in my discussions of Coleridge and Keats. A final debt, here as in so much that I have written, is to Alfred North Whitehead, whose high-mindedness and generosity of vision are one of the finest things I have ever had the luck to experience. It was he who taught me to think not only of this particular problem, but of this general kind of problem, with the confidence that what is most directly and personally relevant to us is also what is most worthy of the highest generality of thought.

W.J.B.

Cambridge, Massachusetts

Contents

I | The Second Temple 1

II | The Neoclassic Dilemma 29

III | The Eighteenth-Century Reconsideration: Hume and the Essential Diagnosis 59

IV | The Third Temple 93

Index 137

I | The Second Temple

Strong were our Syres; and as they Fought they Writ,
Conqu'ring with force of Arms, and dint of Wit;
Theirs was the Gyant Race, before the Flood;
And thus, when *Charles* return'd, our Empire stood.

. . .

Our Age was cultivated thus at length;
But what we gain'd in skill we lost in strength.
Our Builders were, with want of Genius, curst;
The Second Temple was not like the first.

—Dryden, "To Mr. Congreve" (1694)

Our subject could be expressed by a remark Samuel Johnson quotes from Pliny in one of the *Rambler* essays (No. 86): "The burthen of government is increased upon princes by the virtues of their immediate predecessors." And Johnson goes on to add: "It is, indeed, always *dangerous* to be placed in a state of unavoidable comparison with excellence, and the danger is still greater when that excellence is consecrated by death . . . He that succeeds a celebrated writer, has the same difficulties to encounter." That word "dangerous" deserves a moment's reflection. In its original, rather ominous sense, it means "having lost one's freedom," having become "dominated" and turned into the position of a household thrall: being placed in jeopardy, subjected to the tyranny of something outside one's own control as a free agent. A cognate is our word "dungeon."

I have often wondered whether we could find any more comprehensive way of taking up the whole of English poetry during the last three centuries – or for that matter the modern history of the arts in general – than by exploring the effects of this accumulating anxiety and the question it so directly presents to the poet or artist: *What is there left to do?* To say that this has always been a problem, and that the arts have still managed to survive, does not undercut the fact that it has become far more pressing in the modern world. Of course the situation is an old one. We need not even start with Rome or Alexandria, those exemplars of what it can mean to the artist to stand in competition with an admired past. We could go back to an almost forgotten Egyptian scribe of 2000 B.C. (Khakheperresenb), who inherited in his literary legacy no Homer, Sophocles, Dante, Shakespeare, Milton, Goethe, or Dickens – no formidable variety of literary genres available in thousands of libraries – yet who still left the poignant epigram: "Would I had phrases that are not known, utterances that are strange, in new language that has not been used, free from repetition, not an utterance which has grown stale, which men of old have spoken." But a problem can become more acute under some conditions than others. And, whatever other generalizations can be made about the arts since the Renaissance, a fact with which we can hardly quarrel – though we instinctively resist some of the implications – is that the means of preserving and distributing the literature (and more recently the other arts) of the past have immeasurably increased, and to such a point that we now have confronting the artist – or have *in potentia* – a vast array of varied achievement, existing and constantly multiplying in an "eternal present."

We could, in fact, argue that the remorseless deepening of self-consciousness, before the rich and intimidating legacy of the past, has become the greatest single problem that modern art (art, that is to say, since the later seventeenth century) has had to face, and that it will become increasingly so in the future. In comparison, many of the ideas or preoccupations (thematic, social, formal, or psychoanalytic) that we extract as aims, interests, conflicts, anxieties, influences, or "background," and then picture as so sharply pressing on the mind of the artist, are less directly urgent. In our own response to a constantly expanding subject matter, we forget that what provides opportunity for us, as critics and historians, may be simultaneously foreclosing – or at least appearing to foreclose – opportunity for the artist, and that, as T. S. Eliot said, "Not only every great poet, but every genuine, though lesser poet, fulfills once for all some possibility of the language, and so leaves one possibility less for his successors." Whatever he may say, or not say, about his predecessors, the poet from Dryden to Eliot has been unavoidably aware of them, and never so much as when he has tried to establish a difference; and he has been keenly and very personally aware of them in a way that he was not, for example (if he was writing in the early eighteenth century), of Newton, Locke, or Shaftesbury. Of course Newtonian philosophy, formal ideals of order and decorum, Shaftesburian benevolence, and many other concepts or interests that we ourselves pursue may all have concerned eighteenth-century poets. It is taken for granted that they have an important place in our consideration of what the English poetry of the eighteenth century became. The point is merely that these poets also had one very direct and practical problem that was at least as absorbing to them, and often far more so: the stark problem of what and how to write.

So with the English Romantics. Keats, who certainly faced enough personal difficulties, would become really despondent only (except after his fatal illness began) when, as he told his friend Richard Woodhouse, he felt that "there was nothing original to be written in poetry; that its riches were already exhausted – and all its beauties forestalled." Goethe rejoiced that he was not born an Englishman and forced to compete with the achievement of Shakespeare. Even if one is writing in another language, said Goethe, "a productive nature ought not to read more than one of Shakespeare's dramas in a year if he would not be wrecked entirely." Direct imitation is obviously not the answer. (Shakespeare, as he says elsewhere, "gives us golden apples in silver dishes." By careful study we may acquire the silver dishes while discovering that we have "only potatoes to put in them.") But attempting – after one knows his works – to proceed differently for the sake of mere difference is even less satisfactory. Goethe became increasingly frank about the matter as he grew older:

> We spoke about English literature [said Eckermann, 2 January 1824], about the greatness of Shakespeare, and what an unlucky position all English dramatic writers have, coming

after that poetic giant. "A dramatic talent," Goethe continued, "if it were significant, could not help taking notice of Shakespeare; indeed, it could not help studying him. But to study him is to become aware that Shakespeare has already exhausted the whole of human nature in all directions and in all depths and heights, and that for those who come after him, there remains nothing more to do. And where would an earnest soul, capable of appreciating genius, find the courage even to set pen to paper, if he were aware of such unfathomable and unreachable excellence already in existence! In that respect I was certainly better off in my dear Germany fifty years ago. I could very soon come to terms with the literature already in existence. It could not impose on me for long, and it could not much hold me back . . . Thus gradually advancing I followed my own natural development . . . And in each stage of my life and development my idea of excellence was never much greater than I was able to attain.

"But had I been born an Englishman, and had those manifold masterworks pressed in upon me with all their power from my first youthful awakening, it would have overwhelmed me, and I would not have known what I wanted to do! I would never have been able to advance with so light and cheerful a spirit, but would certainly have been obliged to consider for a long time and look about me in order to find some new expedient."

The situation is the same when we move on to the Victorians and especially to the first half of the twentieth century. These writers, we say, were faced with a difficult situation, which we then proceed to document — the decline of faith, the lack of certainty in moral as well as religious values. All this is true (and is true of certain earlier eras). But the pessimism we explain with such a cumbersome machinery of ideas has often an even sharper, more immediate spur: the nagging questions, what is there left to write? and how, as craftsmen, do we get not only new subjects but a new idiom? A great deal of modern literature — and criticism — is haunted, as Stephen Spender says, by the thought of a "Second Fall of Man," and almost everything has been blamed: the Renaissance loss of the medieval unity of faith, Baconian science, British empiricism, Rousseau, the French Revolution, industrialism, nineteenth-century science, universities and academicism, the growing complexity of ordinary life, the spread of mass media. But whatever else enters into the situation, the principal explanation is the writer's loss of self-confidence as he compares what he feels able to do with the rich heritage of past art and literature. Scientists, we notice, are not affected by this despondency, at least not yet. And we do not account for that very interesting difference, or for any number of other differences, if we try to attribute it to mere insensitivity.

—2—

Yet this is not a subject we have been much tempted to pursue, at least during the last century — though it is precisely during this period, and particularly the last fifty years, that the psychological complexities we have in mind have begun to thicken in Malthusian progression.

Why is it that we fight shy of the problem, and, in our vast annual output of commentary on the arts, prefer to devote our energies to almost any or every other topic or approach? There seem to me several explanations. The critic, biographer, or historian, in his consideration of the arts, has by definition a different vocation (though we need not remind ourselves of the fact itself, we occasionally need to remind ourselves of some of its implications); and in his own personal experience the situation we mention does not press home to him to the same degree or in the same way. He may have his own anxieties and competitions in the face of previous achievement, and these may certainly cripple rather than inspire him in his own range and magnanimity as a humanist. But the accumulation of past work from which he may feel tempted or even forced to differ in order to secure identity (whether through increasing specialism in smaller corners, through more general forms of reinterpretation, or through mere quibble) is chronologically far more limited. It is primarily the product of the last fifty years. Moreover, there is a difference in kind as well as degree. In one way especially the "literature of knowledge" – of fact and expository discussion – will always differ, as De Quincey said, from the "literature of power" and the other arts. The discovery of even a handful of new facts, the correction of some others, or even the mere ability to rearrange details or arguments with some ingenuity for debate or supplement, will permit the writing, again and again, of a new work. In short, the "literature of knowledge" with its expository discussion is, even at its best, "provisional" and can always be superseded. But the *Iliad* or *King Lear* will not be dislodged with the same ease or excuse. They are, as De Quincey said, "finished and unalterable" – like every other work of art, however minor. To feel constraints in competition with even the greatest scholars and critics of the last fifty years is not, in other words, the same thing as to be in competition with Michelangelo, Shakespeare, Rembrandt, Bach, Beethoven, Dickens, or Mann and with the finalities that the works of such men present.

Relatively free from immediate personal experience of the same sort, we continue to remain oblivious because of the natural pride and embarrassed silence of the writer himself. The writer or artist may be self-revealing enough in other ways. But when his anxiety has to do with the all-important matter of his craft, and his achievement or fear of impotence there, he naturally prefers to wrestle with it privately or to express it only indirectly. The subject, in other words, is not one for which we can compile a clean-cut reading list. We begin to sense its importance only when we look between the lines, or follow closely the life of writer after writer, or weigh the context of self-defensive manifestoes or fatalistic excuses in eras of militant transition in style, and, above all, when we note the nagging apprehension, from generation to generation, that the poet is somehow becoming increasingly powerless to attain (or is in some way being forbidden to try to attain) the scope and power of the earlier poetry that he so deeply admires.

But there is something else, to which we are quick to apply the word *taboo* when we confront it in others instead of ourselves. The confidence of the artist and the humanist generally has not been at one of its historical peaks during our own period. We have become very defensive, and to that extent participate in the rigidities of defense. We become especially disturbed at any speculation that would even suggest, at first glance, that what we value so highly, what we spend so much time discussing and teaching, may have taken the turns it has in the past, and may be assuming the forms that it does in our own period, because of an essential (possibly inevitable) retrenchment. We can take in our stride general theories of decline. If they are extreme enough, as in Spengler's *Decline of the West,* we are confident that we can pick holes in them. And if we find them current in some earlier period, we do not stop to ask whether they had some objective justification but deal with them as curious asides, fashionable notions, or the result of reading some earlier theorist. (Goldsmith and others in the English eighteenth century who thought the arts were moving into a less vital stage had — we say — read Vico, or had at least read or talked with someone else who had read Vico.) Or if, as biographers, we are considering writers like Coleridge or Keats, we dissolve their inner anxieties about what the poet is still able to do, within other, more personal forms of reductionism: Coleridge was struggling again with opium or his neuroses generally; Keats was having trouble with Fanny Brawne or memories of his dead parents, and was therefore having his own pessimistic moments.

But if we are confronted with the suggestion that one age of achievement in the arts may necessarily — because of its greatness, and because of the incorrigible nature of man's mind — force a search for difference, even though that difference means a retrenchment, we become uneasy. When the change in the arts since the Renaissance is attributed to the loss of religious faith, to the growth of science, to commercialism, or to the development of mass media, we are always at liberty to feel that those circumstances may conceivably change again. But the deepest fear we have is of the mind of man itself, primarily because of its dark unpredictabilities, and with them the possibility that the arts could, over the long range, be considered as by definition suicidal: that, given the massive achievement in the past, they may have no further way to proceed except toward progressive refinement, nuance, indirection, and finally, through the continued pressure for difference, into the various forms of anti-art.

The speculation that this may be so — or that the modern spirit is beginning, rightly or wrongly, to believe that it is so — is a major theme of one of the most disturbing novels of our century, Thomas Mann's *Dr. Faustus*. We find the implications so unsettling, in this modern version of the Faust legend, that we naturally prefer — if we can be brought to linger on the book rather than forget it — to stress other themes, other implications that can be more localized (for instance, the condition of Germany between the two World Wars). For Mann's twentieth-century Faustus, a German composer of genius, all the most fruitful possibilities in music have already been so brilliantly exploited that nothing is now left for the art except a parody of itself and of its past — a self-mockery, technically accomplished but spiritually dead in hope, in short, an "aristocratic nihilism." It is "anti-art" in the sense of art turning finally against itself. And this modern Dr. Faustus, so cerebral and self-conscious before the variety and richness of what has already been done, sells his soul to the devil – as in the old Faust legend – in order to be able once again to produce great art. The special horror is that this involves the willing, the deliberately chosen, destruction of part of his brain in order to free himself from the crippling inhibitions of self-consciousness – a partial destruction of the brain that is to be followed, after the agreed lapse of years, by what he knows beforehand will be a complete disintegration.

The universality of the problem lies in the fact that the arts, in addition to everything else that can be said of them, are also the sensitive antennae of human life generally; that as with them so, in time, with everything else that we still subsume by the word "culture" (however inadequate the word – but we have no other shorthand term). If what is implied in Mann's fable is or even could be true, or half-true, then what of man's situation in general as he is now beginning to face, and will face increasingly, the potential self-division forced upon him by his growing literacy and sophistication – his knowledge about himself, his past, the immense variety of what has been done and said, all brought with immediate focus and pressure, like a huge inverted pyramid, upon the naked moment, the short flicker, of any one individual life? The self-division arises because, except in the cumulative sciences, where a step-by-step use of deliberately specialized effort can be harnessed, the weight of everything else that has been done, said, or exemplified cannot, in conscience, be wholly denied, though on the other hand there is the natural desire of every human being to assert himself in such time as he has – to contribute in some respect, however small, or, if he cannot contribute, to leave his mark in some other way.

—3—

We may feel less naked, less prey to existential *Angst* and helplessness, if we know that we have not been condemned by history to be the first to face this frightful challenge, unique though it is, in scale, to the modern world. There may be some comfort to our feeling of historical loneliness – and not only comfort but some spur to both our courage and potentialities for good sense – to know we have a predecessor in the eighteenth century, a century that serves as the essential crossroad between all that we imply when we use the word "Renaissance" and much of what we mean when we speak of the "modern." We are only beginning to understand this about the eighteenth century, and to realize how much, in our approach to it and to all that which, in Johnson's phrase, can be "put to use," we have still lingered in the suburbs of its significance – above all, its significance for us now as contrasted with that which it had, or seemed to have, for the nineteenth century. With the nineteenth and the greater part of the twentieth century behind us, the eighteenth has long ceased to be something from which we need to disengage ourselves. We are now free to concentrate less on what differentiates it from ourselves and more on what we share. For us now, looking back on the last four centuries as a whole, the central interest of the eighteenth century is that it is the first period in modern history to face the problem of what it means to come *immediately* after a great creative achievement. It was the first to face what it means to have already achieved some of the ends to which the modern (that is, the Renaissance) spirit had at the beginning aspired. Simultaneously, we have the start of almost everything else we associate with the modern world – the attempted Europeanization of the globe, with some of its new embarrassments; the American and French Revolutions; the rapid spread of literacy; the beginning of industrialism, urbanization, and the sudden rapid increase of population; and, in its later half, the creation of most of what we associate with the premises of the modern effort not only in the arts but in philosophy.

What is so reassuring to us, as we look back on this astonishing century now and begin to learn more about it with the kind of perspective just mentioned, is its union of strength (good sense, even shrewdness and worldliness) with openness and generous empathy for all that William James implied when he spoke of literature and the arts as the "tender-minded pursuits." What is so reassuring is that here, if nowhere else, all that we ourselves prize (or should like, if we were bold enough, to say that we prize) in the "tender-minded" is taken for granted as valuable, as indeed supremely valuable, while at the same time we have as "tough-minded" a group of champions for the sympathetic and the humane as, in our most desperate moments, we could ever have hoped for. As we look further into this century, which produced, in David Hume, the greatest skeptic in the history of philosophy but which also produced Mozart and Beethoven and Burke, we feel a growing confidence about what can be "put to use."

This is also true of our special problem here — the whole problem of the "burden of the past" as it applies to the arts (and, by implication, to humanistic interests and pursuits as a whole). My thought, in these lectures, is twofold: to pose for us, in general, this central problem — to express the hope that we can pluck it out into the open and to try to see it for what it is — and, second, to help us reground ourselves, to get a clearer idea of our bearings, by looking back with a fresh eye to the beginning drama of what we ourselves are now living with and feel so deep a need to bring into perspective. In using the word "drama" I am thinking not only of the variety in voice and stance (realistic, sentimental, nostalgic, prejudiced, imaginative, worldly, analytic, sociological, aesthetic, moral) but also of the trauma – and there was one in this massive self-reconsideration – and of its uneasy but brilliantly creative resolutions.

—4—

But first we must narrow our focus, and, leaving broader generalities aside, concentrate on what the eighteenth-century poet inherited. This involves lingering, at least for a moment, on what for half a century we have called "neoclassicism." In what I am saying now, I am trying to focus especially on England, and not merely on England but on the poet and the situation of the poet. And this further involves freeing ourselves from some of the tyranny of abstractions and labels, and of our post-Hegelian urge to give them body, so that we can use them rather than be used by them.

If we took up English neoclassicism solely in the light of what we call the history of ideas, it could still remain one of the great unresolved puzzles of literary history. No explanation for it – at least no explanation why it caught on so quickly and firmly after 1660 – would satisfy anyone for very long except the person who provided it.

Let me hurry to say that I am not speaking of English neoclassic *theory* – that is, of neoclassic *critical* writing. It is only too easy, if we confine ourselves to the history of critical theory, to trace an ancestral line through Sir Philip Sidney and Ben Jonson down to the Restoration (the history of critical theory is by definition a history of ideas). And if we want more help, we have merely to turn to the intellectual history of England during the sixteenth and seventeenth centuries and we can find any number of ideas, if not ancestral, at least collateral, to enrich our genealogical chart. But once the glow of discovery has faded, the result is not really very persuasive except to the confirmed

Hegelian, of whom we should remember that there are twentieth- as well as nineteenth-century varieties. Our consciences begin to remind us that, as historians of ideas, we are naturally swayed by special interests. We have a vocational interest in presupposing that there is a relatively clean-cut influence of ideas on artists — meaning, by "ideas," concepts that we, as historians, have abstracted from a large, diverse period of human life, which may very well have struck our attention only because they are so susceptible of genealogy. Of course we all say — and say it quite sincerely — that what we are really interested in is the *reciprocal* influence of ideas and art. But it is so difficult to put neatly the influence of art, in all its diversity, on the climate of ideas! To the orderly mind of the historian, this task is as elusive, or as unmanageably messy, as having to describe and categorize the influence of people on ideas. We find ourselves feeling that it is better to leave all that for some future, more leisurely consideration. Hence, in our actual practice if not in ultimate ideal, we lean toward the simplicities of thinking in terms of a one-way traffic.

A sense of all this begins to nag the conscience after we trace our genealogies of ideas in order to explain English neoclassicism: the rephrasing, by sixteenth- and seventeenth-century critics, of classical ideals; the premium on decorum, refinement, regularity, and the ways in which they are particularized; the confidence in method; the influence of mathematics. Are these ideas, these concepts and values that we have abstracted, not progenitors after all of the actual neoclassic literature to come but only midwives, escorts, even (to quote Eliot) "attendant persons"? Putting it another way: would these particular concepts and ideas have been left undeveloped, have fallen on deaf ears, unless there had also been *other* considerations, equally or perhaps more important?

We know very well, for example, that English literature

itself, from the time of Elizabeth down into the mid-seventeenth century, showed a diversity that had been unrivaled since the most fertile days of Athens. We also know that at its best it showed a power or intensity in its diversity (in idiom, in metaphor, in cadence) that has haunted English literature ever since that time. And this literature was written at exactly the same time as those theoretical works to which we are looking for the ancestry of English neoclassicism. We know that the intensity and diversity of that literature (or, putting it more truthfully, an intensity both of and within diversity) far outweigh our thin sketch of theoretical or merely critical concepts through the Elizabethan and Jacobean eras. To put it bluntly: it is not at all from English life and English experience in its widest sense, from the time of Elizabeth through that of Cromwell, that a really developed neoclassicism came so suddenly. We know perfectly well that systematized and pervasive neoclassicism is very much a French product, and that it was in fact viewed as that (whether with respect, restiveness, or antagonism) by the English themselves, from Dryden, Rymer, and Temple down to Hazlitt and Francis Jeffrey a century and a half later.

Then why did English neoclassicism occur? We are always being reminded that these values of the "new classicism" of France never sat too easily on the English mind. Of course they did not. In fact, they were always being qualified by native English attitudes; and (though we have recently tended to exaggerate the amount) there was a good deal of open dissent. But this makes the matter all the more curious: why should it have flourished so rapidly when there was this much tendency to dissent and qualify?

There is, in fact, nothing else in the whole of the long literary history of England quite like this brisk transition. There is no other instance, after the invention of printing, where you find a settled group of literary premises and aims imported almost bodily, adopted with such dispatch, and then transformed into orthodoxy, or near-orthodoxy, for so long a time (a full seventy or eighty years), despite a large undercurrent that runs counter to it. Of the three really great transitions in English poetry since the Elizabethans and Jacobeans, this is the first. The second is found in the large shift that took place in the late eighteenth and early nineteenth centuries, and the third is the radical change of idiom and mode during the first half of the twentieth century. But the second of these transitions, to which we apply the loose word "Romantic," was the reverse in almost every way of what we are considering now. To begin with, it was slower and longer prepared for in the actual writing (as distinct from critical theory) that preceded it. It emerged from within the neoclassic stronghold, opening the walls one by one. To a large extent it was demonstrably — even dramatically — a nationalistic movement in England (as it was in another, more pronounced way in Germany). When we turn to our own era, we have to admit that the transition to the new poetic idiom of the early and middle twentieth century was almost as rapid, and that it was analogous to the neoclassic transition in speed as well as in other ways. On the other hand, this radical modern change was less metaphysically rationalized; in some ways it was closer to its own immediate past (the English Romantics) than Pope ever was to Shakespeare or Milton; nor was it — despite the influence of the French Symbolists and others — a Continental importation: too much else, by that time, was already going on within the English-speaking world generally.

—5—

To the England of the Restoration and the early eighteenth century, the mature and sophisticated neoclassicism of France had an irresistible appeal. It gave the English poet a chance to be different from his immediate predecessors while at the same time it offered a counter-ideal that was impressively, almost monolithically, systematized. French neoclassicism appeared to have answers ready for almost any kind of objection to it. And most of the answers had this further support: they inevitably referred – or pulled the conscience back – to the premises of "reason" and of ordered nature that the English themselves were already sharing, though not perhaps in the same spirit as the French. To dismiss an argument that led directly back to "reason" was something they were not at all prepared to do. It was like attacking virtue itself. Even the most articulate writers who might feel hesitations (for example the group appropriately called, in England as well as France, the *je ne sais quoi* critics) still lacked the vocabulary to express any effective alternative. And in any case, had not England's own Sir Isaac Newton already helped to disclose the universal architecture, and to an extent that no Frenchman had done? – Newton, as James Thomson later said, "whom God / To mortals lent to trace his boundless works."

In addition they had ready to hand the central neoclassic concept of *decorum* – of "propriety" or "what is fitting." In almost every way (ancestry, centrality, potential range of application) its credentials as both an aim and working premise were superb. Its origin was the ancient Greek and specifically Aristotelean conception of the function of art as a unified, harmonious imitation of an ordered nature. As, in the process of nature itself, the parts interrelate through universal, persisting forms and principles, so art in its own particular medium (words, sounds, or visual shapes) seeks to duplicate that process, but at the same time to stress or to highlight it. Hence art concentrates, even more than we in our ordinary experience do, on the general form – selecting only what contributes directly to the particular end (or form) and rejecting what does not. As such, poetry is more "philosophical," as Aristotle said, than a straightforward factual narrative. It is, in short, closer to the "ideal," but "ideal" in the original sense in Greek – in the intellectual perception of pattern, form, and general meaning. *Decorum* applies to the *relevance* or *fitness* of every part to the whole in this "ideal" and admittedly foreshortened selection, which permits a finished and rounded totality. Given its success in art, we have not only unity and cleanliness of form (and with them finish and completeness) but intellectual range and pertinence: cousinship at least (in its best moments something approaching the fraternal) to the process of nature itself when nature is viewed with a philosophical selectivity that focuses not on its accidental details but on its persisting forms.

Extensively and ingeniously developed throughout two centuries of critical thinking, and applied to every aspect of subject and style, the neoclassic concept of decorum was – at least in its more general significance – one of the most difficult premises in the history of art with which to quarrel theoretically. Never before in the West since classical antiquity (hardly at any time even then), and certainly never again after the mid-eighteenth century, has there been available for the poet or artist generally and also for the critic or philosopher, or for anyone who wanted to say anything about the arts, a concept that could potentially fulfill so many functions. It not only could serve as an active hinge between the theory of art and the actual practice of it, but could lead directly to moral and social values and, further, to nature itself and the cosmic order.

Yet in one important way the neoclassic conception of decorum, however theoretically persuasive, carried with it an historical, if not logical, limitation, though we should remember that limitation need not be synonymous with disadvantage or weakness. It was itself an extrapolation that had been made, argued, and embellished, first of all, in the face of the challenge of an admired past, and then contemporaneously in competition with a brilliantly creative present. It had evolved in the early 1500's as a by-product of the more general effort of the European Renaissance to rival the challenge it found in its haunting dream of classical antiquity, and, in this particular case, to do so by concentrating, strictly and analytically, upon what seemed to be the formal essentials in the classical achievement. Moreover, within a generation it was also in active rivalry (which did not of course preclude occasional and even fruitful agreement) with the inventive originality and diversity of Renaissance art and literature themselves. As with almost any ideal extrapolated and militantly defended, it quickly became centripetal rather than centrifugal or diluted. This process seems especially to occur with ideals that have to do with combination and balance of different elements. (One thinks of what has happened to the classical ideal of "temperance," meaning harmonious or rhythmic proportion — "keeping time [*tempus*]" as in music. It has not meant that to most people for quite a while.) If the premise is that every part of a work of art should contribute directly to the whole — that what is especially wanted is unity of impact, unity of focus and significance — it is always tempting to proceed to such an end (at least the "unity" if not the "impact" and "significance") by exclusion. Indeed, for frail human nature the use of exclusion or denial is immensely seductive as the answer to most problems, including moral and social ones. It is always easier, as Johnson said, to throw out or forbid than to incorporate — "to take away superfluities than to supply defects." In the title of George Granville's *Essay upon Unnatural Flights in Poetry* (1701), with all that it suggests, we sense the relief that neoclassic theory could provide: something still remained to be done, and the difficulties were not insuperable.

In the very limitation, in other words, lay much of the attraction. ("No one unable to limit himself," said Boileau, "has ever been able to write.") If in our quick summary we appear to belittle, we should remind ourselves that what we are saying can apply to any formalism that is deliberately exclusive (as opposed to the necessary exclusions in primitive arts), and especially if it is a formalism trying to free itself from, or establish itself after, a strongly emotional and richly mimetic (that is, "realistic") art. We have only to think of the immense effort of the arts, including music, of the early and middle twentieth century to get the nineteenth century off their backs. So strenuous – at times single-minded – was the effort that, during the childhood and youth of those of us now middle-aged, many of us began to assume that the first requirement of the sophisticated poet, artist, or composer was to be as unlike his nineteenth-century predecessors as possible. We even had moments when we suspected that the principal influence on modern poetry, for example, was not so much the array of abstractions cited in the recondite search for aim or justification, but rather the poetry of Tennyson. What we are trying desperately to be unlike can tell a great deal about not only what we are doing but why, and a movement may often be better understood by what it concretely opposes than by its theoretical slogans. In short, this is a situation in which we ourselves have directly shared, and when we confront something like it in other periods we should be able to approach it with some empathy if not with the most fervent applause.

—6—

If Restoration England, through its delayed but now ready embrace of the neoclassic mode, at once secured standards that permitted it to avoid competition with the literature of the immediate past, this was especially because it could do so with that authority (in this case classical antiquity) which is always pleasing to have when you can invoke it from a distant (and therefore "purer") source; pleasing because it is not an authority looming over you but, as something ancestral rather than parental, is remote enough to be more manageable in the quest for your own identity – more open to what the heart wants to select or the imagination to remold. For that matter, the ancestral permitted one – by providing a "purer," more time-hallowed, more conveniently malleable example – even to disparage the parent in the name of "tradition." And in the period from 1660 to about 1730 there were plenty of people ready to snatch this opportunity. If their ranks did not include the major minds and artists, there were enough of them to justify us in recognizing this as the first large-scale example, in the modern history of the arts, of the "leapfrog" use of the past for authority or psychological comfort: the leap over the parental – the principal immediate predecessors – to what Northrop Frye calls the "modal grandfather." (So the English Romantics later invoked the Elizabethans and Jacobeans against their own immediate predecessors. Another century later T. S. Eliot was to invoke the "metaphysical poets" as the prototype of the genuine English "tradition" from which poetry had since strayed.)

It should be emphasized that we are not speaking of the taste of the reading public generally. For example, Milton was probably the most popular major poet for eighteenth-century England. The period saw over a hundred editions of *Paradise Lost,* and over seventy of the complete poems.* This very fact could illustrate our argument that the neoclassic mode, in its stricter and more organized sense, was not the response to a general and popular shift of taste that it is sometimes described as being, but rather an elitist movement in which the incentives were primarily appli-

* See the remark of the German writer K. P. Moritz, below, p. 70.

cable to the condition of the writer himself. We have seen the same thing in twentieth-century formalism. Despite the enormous critical effort to ground it on premises and values that human beings generally — or at least the more educated — are said to be in need of appreciating, the fact remains that the essential appeals of the movement have been to the artist or to those who professionally consider themselves his guardians. (The split between "popular" and "sophisticated" art has always existed in cultivated societies, but it has become progressively greater since the seventeenth century. Of special interest is the growth since then, among intellectuals, of the number that deplore this split, look back nostalgically to happier and simpler eras before it occurred, and yet, while championing the "popular" so long as it is remote enough — Yeats's Celtic mythology, for example — side with the elitist or sophisticated against the "popular" as soon as we come to anything post-Renaissance and above all post-romantic.)

But to return to the situation: it was possible to go still further than reducing your immediate predecessors to size or manageability. You could turn, if you wished, against the ancestral source itself and demonstrate — methodically, indeed legalistically — that even classical antiquity had failed sufficiently to develop its own premises. This is precisely what happened in the still famous "quarrel of the Ancients and the Moderns" that flourished in seventeenth-century France and then seeded itself in Restoration England, though there the soil proved less promising. With the Ancients themselves being weighed in the balance and found wanting because they were not "correct" enough, the liberals began to align themselves in defense of the Ancients. So, in Swift's burlesque of the quarrel in his *Battle of the Books*, he uses the bee as the symbol of the Ancients and the spider of the Moderns. The bee, turning directly to what is outside of us (nature), brings home honey and wax, thus furnishing man with both "sweetness and light." The spider, by contrast, is a domestic creature, working within a shorter radius, indeed preferring a corner. The tireless weaving of rule and regulation that Swift is attacking in the Moderns, far from being the product of a direct and far-ranging use of "nature," is spun subjectively from the spider's own body, and the web – at once systematic and flimsy – is capable only of catching dirt and insects. The interest of the "quarrel of the Ancients and the Moderns" is that of all good comedy – potential universality (if possible, a relevance close enough to threaten) and, for the audience, detachment. The detachment is provided for us by historical distance: the *particular* issues, taking this particular form, are no longer there and we can view them without partisanship and self-defense. The universality lies in the fact that, though the special issues are now distant to the point of triviality, the motives, the procedures, are not. Human nature, as Johnson said, is in general more inclined to censure than to praise. Add to this that almost every writer finds it "not only difficult but disagreeable" to dwell on things "really and naturally great." He becomes "degraded in his own eyes by standing in comparison with his own subject, to which he can hope to add nothing." If he cannot contribute his mite, he feels that he can at least secure importance by withholding it.

But the major writers, to repeat, are found in neither group – those who turned against the parental or (least of all) against the ancestral. It was not Dryden but the almost forgotten Charles Gildon who wrote "For the Modern Poets against the Ancients" (1694) and described the new spirit of strict regulation and analysis as "more essential to Poetry than any other Art or Science" – more essential since poetry, left to itself, is so incorrigibly open to varied human interests. Nor was it Pope but poor William Guthrie who boasted of modern "dramatic poetry" – especially tragedy – that it at last "stands upon the same footing as our noble system of Newtonian philosophy." Pope, so quick to ridicule such remarks, had himself simply turned to other forms of writing, and, however self-defensive in more personal ways, without militance.

Indeed, one of the paradoxes of what we have been describing is that the pressure of the "burden of the past" was felt most sharply by the major writers and artists, if only because they had the intelligence to see where their opportunities lay; and it is they who set the tone for the new formal style, the new mode, and the genres associated with the period, especially satire and the verse essay. Yet it was also they who were least blithe or slapdash in disposing of, or downgrading, their predecessors. True, they might occasionally, forgivably, cluck the tongue or shake the finger about particular details. But this was not the same thing. In a deeper way than others, they knew how much was involved.

It was not at all the confidence of "superiority" so loudly proclaimed by others that sustained them as they developed one of the greatest formal poetic styles the English language has yet seen, the finest comic and satiric writing in modern literature, and a prose never excelled in English before and rarely since. It was, as we said, a realization of where the opportunities lay at this particular time. Had the circumstances been different, they took it for granted that they would have written differently. As Dryden said about the use of rhyme in dramatic tragedy (speaking through Neander in the *Essay of Dramatic Poesy*), this was one of the ways of writing that Shakespeare and his contemporaries had not exploited; and, far from implying adverse criticism of what they had done, the attempt to turn to other modes of writing now was a tribute. It involved the recognition that "there is scarce an humor, a character, or any kind of plot which they have not used." Would they themselves, after so rich an expenditure of all that could be done in the art, have been able to "equal themselves, were they to rise and write again?" We "acknowledge them our fathers," but they have already spent their estates before these "came to their children's hand." As a result our present choice is "either not to write at all, or to attempt some other way."

—7—

What Dryden is saying here – and all that it implies – is something with which he continued to live throughout his career, and with the good-natured sanity that every later professional man of letters has admired. The thought deepened as the years passed and as he saw his own work, and what the years since the Restoration had been able to do, with increasing perspective. Looking back upon the writers before the Restoration, he describes them now as the "giant race before the flood" – before the great change to the modern formalism. In lines written near the end of his life to his friend William Congreve (1694), congratulating Congreve on a new comedy, he generously pretends that with this new play "the promised hour has come at last; / The present Age of Wit obscures the past." The gentle irony, in so large a claim, is as obvious as the obsession of the period with the achievement of the past. And the fascination of the poem is that the strongest lines, within this formal proscenium arch of conventional compliment, express his own personal condition in his old age, or undercut the clichés of the new formalism ("your *least* Praise is be Regular"), or, above all, speak of the relation of the age itself to that preceding:

> Strong were our Syres; and as they Fought they Writ,
> Conqu'ring with force of Arms, and dint of Wit;
> Theirs was the Gyant Race, before the Flood;
> And thus, when *Charles* Return'd, our Empire stood.

With the Restoration, he goes on, the "stubborn Soil" was "manur'd," and through the new "Rules of Husbandry" the weeds were cut and the rank growth brought into cleaner form:

> Our Age was cultivated thus at length;
> But what we gain'd in skill we lost in strength.
> Our Builders were, with want of Genius, curst;
> The Second Temple was not like the First.

The Second Temple, completed seventy years after the destruction of the First by Nebuchadnezzar, differed in four ways especially from the Temple of Solomon. Though about the same in area, it was not so high. It was also less of a unit, being divided now into an outer and inner court. In equipment and decoration it was barer. Above all, the Holy of Holies was now an empty shrine, as it was also to remain in the magnificent Third Temple built by Herod. The Ark of the Covenant was gone, and no one felt at liberty to try to replace it with a substitute.

II | The Neoclassic Dilemma

In confronting a brilliantly creative achievement immediately before him in his own language, different from the mode he himself was to exploit, Dryden's situation as a seventeenth-century poet was almost unique. He is the first great European (not merely English) example of a major writer who is taking it for granted that the very existence of a past creates the necessity for difference – not for the audience, not *sub specie aeternitatis,* but for the writer or artist himself. It is typical of both his good sense and his courage as an artist – indeed one of the marks of his greatness – that he felt no defensive need to argue otherwise.

So with Dryden's successor, Alexander Pope, who for English poetic style so masterfully continued and perfected the new mode that Johnson felt any further concentration and "refinement" in this direction would be "dangerous." Pope knew very well what he was doing. Of his list of the English poets who seemed to him greatest, only one (Dryden) was in his own special tradition. But the early advice of William Walsh remained with him, nor did Pope – certainly one of the eight or ten most gifted poets in the entire history of English letters – have any reason to be ashamed of the result in following it: "Mr. Walsh . . . used to tell me that there was *one way left of excelling*; for though we had several great poets, we never had any one great poet that was *correct*; and he desired me to make that my study and aim."

In short it was not the *premises* of neoclassic formalism that by themselves produced the first radical and sudden change in the history of English poetic style. It was the need to use them in the way that they were used. Significantly, the musical composer was still free from this particular problem, though the same theoretical premises were there. The reason is simply that previous works of music were not yet collected, not yet eulogized, studied, or discussed with the same close knowledge. Hence a composer like Handel was able to write as prolifically and rapidly as he did, appropriating, as freely as Shakespeare, whatever he chose. The *Messiah,* with all its complexity, could thus be turned out in less than a month, with no inhibition, no sense of a need to fight shy of range, variety, or the "sublime" and to concentrate instead on polishing one special mode. A tenth of Handel's vast output would have made the reputation of a composer forced two centuries later to prove his difference and identity step by step or bar by bar. Nor was much of it mere filler. Beethoven devoted his last days to reading the scores of Handel. What we are saying of Handel is equally true of Bach and the major composers generally throughout the eighteenth century. The point is that, where there was inhibition or retrenchment in the arts, the theoretical premises, however strict, were not the cause, though they could be overwhelmingly persuasive if one was prepared to accept them; and that, when inhibition or retrenchment occurred, there were other, more directly personal reasons.

—2—

It is necessary to repeat that what we are saying is in no way intended to disparage the result, and there is no reason for the scholar or critic who devotes himself to the study and interpretation of it to become more hotly defensive than were Dryden and Pope themselves in their own conception that what they were building or completing was a "Second Temple," which "was not like the First."

We are speaking of a state of mind — and a state of mind of which the neoclassic experience is only the first major example. The "late-comer" — to use Sainte-Beuve's term in "What Is a Classic?" — may be expected to have the feelings and situation of a "late-comer." And not to recognize this is only to underestimate what was actually done.

The neoclassic achievement may be taken for granted. In fact it is hard to imagine what literature and art would have been, after the middle seventeenth century, without the centripetal concentration it provided – and not merely for a century or so. In all probability we should have had the long centrifugal disintegration – the progressive nuancing of detail and manner – that follows any large movement in the arts when a clear-cut alternative is lacking, endowed with comparable authority and providing the sanction or justification that the arts, even in rebellion, instinctively crave.

Finally, the greatness of the neoclassic achievement is underlined by the fact that, as compared with almost every major movement since then, its leading minds were honestly and realistically aware of their situation and of what they were doing. As a result they were able to be self-corrective, able to reconsider and revise, even before the eighteenth century was half over, their entire mode and approach, and in the process to create what, extending Dryden's metaphor, we could call the "Third Temple" – the third great movement in modern (post-medieval) Western art and literature.

This is something of an accomplishment: to have carried through the perfection of one major mode of art and thinking, and at the same time to have created its successor. The persisting myopia of compartmentalized literary studies, especially English literary studies, is constantly seducing us into forgetting that Kant, Beethoven, Goethe, Schiller, Blake, Wordsworth, Coleridge – not to mention many others that we routinely associate with the "nineteenth century" – were all born and educated, and in some cases produced their major works, in the eighteenth century. The youth that a period produces, educates, and brings to maturity is very much a part of what that period is.

—3—

From the start a major dilemma confronted the neoclassic effort, and one by no means to its discredit. The essential strength of the movement lay in its firm hold on the classical (or at first a selective conception of the classical) as a prototype of what still remained to be done. But it also faced the risk of being hoist with its own petard. It is one thing to weigh our immediate predecessors against the classical model (a model extracted from the best of eight centuries, with most of the dross removed, and rendered still more compact and formidable through further centuries of study and eulogy) and then to find our predecessors wanting, at least in some respects. But it is another thing to find that the same standard is now to be applied to ourselves, and to our actual performance rather than just our proclaimed aspirations.

The risk was naturally greatest for the poet or the artist, always so much more vulnerable than the theorist; and it is the poet with whom we are principally concerned. But it was shared by the whole movement, and increasingly recognized by it as the classical was reconsidered and as the French neoclassic and its English "Augustan" counterpart began to assume perspective, to take their contours from reality rather than ambition or hope. Before the first third of the eighteenth century was over, it was plain that, by having handed over the conscience so wholeheartedly to the classical ideal, the neoclassic effort was faced with a situation that it could live happily neither with nor without. The gains were enormous in every other aspect of life — intellectual, social, political. Values were quickly incorporated, explicated, developed, popularized, that brought the European world (and the new Europe overseas) into a healthful, badly needed equilibrium, and that then, almost as quickly, began to open up avenues in every direction, which the nineteenth-century world was to exploit further. The gain in the arts was obvious too. There would otherwise have been no "Second Temple" at all but only a patchy cleaning of remnants or a rebuilding of cubicles on the site of the First Temple: refinements, for example, on Cowley, and those odes of his that had begun to seem like platters of hors d'oeuvres. But still there was something missing – and did not the major poets themselves admit it indirectly?

The truth is that like Scripture, or like any other comprehensive body of ideals, the classical can always be used for more than one purpose. If we can invoke it to help us in taking a particular stand (especially one in the name of form, order, or sanity – qualities associated almost by definition with the classical, and especially revered as such during the long adolescence of postclassical Europe), there is also much that can be cited against us as soon as we begin to specialize too purely or narrowly within what we think is the classical example. Hence the classical so often proves a Trojan Horse when more restricted movements in the arts try to embrace and incorporate it for authority. More than what is wanted at the start inevitably emerges, and in time the gates of the city are reopened.

Once the effort to reform – to give a "new form" to or simply to cap – the Renaissance achievement was really under way, other qualities of the classical (Greek now rather than Roman) returned by the middle of the eighteenth century to haunt the cultivated imagination: the great classical ideal of the moral function of art, and poetry in particular – poetry as an educator of the mind and emotions; the range of appeal in the audience it had touched and should touch; the range of genres – epic, tragedy, and on down through the "lesser" types; the strong, widely shared national involvement in poetry and the other arts; the variety of characters portrayed in epic and dramatic form; the emotional immediacy of language;

the imaginative strength of metaphor. Above all there was "originality" – the power of "invention"; and, as Pope said in beginning the preface to his translation of the *Iliad* (1715), it is "invention" that especially "distinguishes all great genius."

This was the dilemma that eighteenth-century neo-classicism inherited, and with which it was to live as it reconsidered its position throughout the remainder of the century. A dilemma, like any other form of challenge, can be fruitful, depending on how we react to it. In fact, if frankly faced, it can be one of the ways by which a movement stays alive, deferring – even avoiding – the senilities of self-congratulation and the irrelevance and thinness of defensive mannerism.

To the eternal credit of the eighteenth century, especially in England, it faced this challenge – as it did so many others in the arts, in philosophy and psychology, in science, and in government – with a union of good sense, honesty, and imaginative resource. In the process it also created the whole modern movement in the arts, of which Romanticism is the first stage. And the great reconsideration of the arts throughout the eighteenth century, especially after 1750, is to a large extent the result of the Jacob-like wrestle of the century with the classical angel, the classical ideal – its attempt to come to terms with that ideal and to secure its blessing.

–4–

At first, in its long wrestle with the classical ideal, the problems seemed manageable. The more positive answers focused on the role of the poet, the new use of classical imitation, and the social conditions of the present age (1660 to about 1730).

Subscribing completely to the classical ideal of the poet and artist as a "teacher," a "legislator *manqué*," the neoclassic apologist could say – and justly – that satire, as a moral or "corrective" form, and didactic poetry were as richly developed now as at any time before. Moreover, however "refined" in versification – and was this not itself a desired classical aim? – poetry had still an "open" idiom: it could be, and was, widely read. Anyone with reasonable intelligence could follow it and receive both pleasure and mental profit, while at the same time there was much in the best poetry to satisfy the most exacting mind. There might not be great epic themes, turning on the marvelous adventures of legendary heroes. But few of us lead such lives, from the peasant to the more sophisticated; and the chances are that few, if any, ever led such lives in the past. Not everything associated with the great works of the remote past needs to be salvaged and described again. The essential point was that poetry, as much as ever, was still "public" – still in keeping with the classical ideal of it as "perfected utterance," as the best possible way of saying anything, and as addressed to a wide audience. True, some of the greater poetry of the period just before, from the Elizabethan period down to Milton, had a wide audience too. But was not much of its "popular" appeal more limited and ephemeral than we now think it was? How many thoughtful men, in government, law, the other professions, read and pondered poetry in the Tudor period with more intellectual relish than was done now? How many such men had there been anyway? In any case, however "refined" the formality and expression of the new mode might be, it was as truly "public" and open as ever, and at the same time the sound, durable models of the classical were now more firmly in mind than before.

Moreover, the new poetry – in fact much of the new art generally – was directly linking arms with the classical, if only as the lesser partner (but was this not praise enough?), through the creative use of *imitation*. Why should not an important part of the subject matter of poetry be its own rich past? And why, when a standard had been established (and it had), should one not try to work in, through, or at least near it rather than to cultivate difference for its own sake? We cannot linger on this particular matter as we should need to do if we were concentrating on the actual poetry of the time. But we may in passing recognize that never before and never thus far since have the use and imitation of past models (classical or other) been more sustained, more thoughtful, more brilliant. When we say "brilliant," we should remember that we must include that more restless brother of Imitation, "Parody." The start of what we think of as the novel in *Don Quixote* and the interplay of "anti-romance" with the parody of classical epic in Fielding during the novel's adolescence should be enough to remind us of the creative uses of imitation and parody. Granted that the greatest success of parody was to be in prose, particularly that of Jonathan Swift. But its importance in poetry is major and fertile, though admittedly for a shorter time.

Finally, when people talked nostalgically of Homer and the ancient world (not to mention Elizabethan England), it could be answered that these are different times. There has been an immense development in societies, whether we think it altogether to the good or not. Given the increasing organization of society, the need for moral improvement (and because we have a higher standard, not because we are more depraved), and the growth of scientific knowledge, should not poetry "adapt" to its own age? This was precisely the argument we were later to hear so strenuously put in the 1920's: that poetry — and art generally — should "adapt" to its age. The difference is that the neoclassic justification focused on what was considered most desirable for the age rather than what was simply thought to mirror it. Hence the familiar Augustan equation of "refinement," polish, form, in the arts — in decorum, proportion, versification, smoothness — with social and individual moral progress, at least as a hope. Granted it could be overdone. We may think here of Dryden's remark, in the poem to Congreve, that "regularity" is the "least" of the praises a poet can have, or of Pope's scornful line about the "correctly cold, and regularly low."

—5—

But before the challenge of what was soon to be called "originality" the neoclassic movement laid down its arms, at least for a while, and raised — quite sensibly — the question whether it was all that important.* Of an observation, we should ask not whether it is "original" but whether it is true. Of a course of action, we should ask whether it is good or at least in accordance with the actuality of things. If our criterion is whether a thing is new or original, we are introducing something entirely extraneous to the real value of the thing. Originality in that sense is always open to an individual: he has only to deny, or to proceed to do the opposite, however capricious or suicidal. This, for fifty years before 1700, had been the considered argument of French neoclassic criticism, repeated with an emphasis that soon began to betray some uneasiness. And it was quickly taken over by the English. "It is impossible for us, who live in the latter ages of the world," said Addison in the *Spectator*, paraphrasing Boileau, "to make observations . . . which have not been touched on by others. We have

* Because we do not find the word itself ("originality" as distinct from the adjective "original") in critical writing until later on, it is often said that the problem never even arose. One can avoid an entire area of concern by looking too myopically for a single word. When Robert Burton states that "we can say nothing but what has been said," or Carew that we have only "the rifled fields" from which all the "buds of invention" have been plucked centuries before, or La Bruyère that we have nothing left before us except servile repetition or "forced conceits" to establish our difference from the past, we are justified in speaking of the concept of what was later to be called "originality."

little else left us but to represent the common sense of mankind in more strong, more beautiful, more uncommon lights." "Nature being still the same," said Steele in the *Guardian*, "it is impossible for any modern writer to paint her otherwise than the ancients have done." And he goes on to suggest that readers could find a new attraction superadded when a modern work revives the memory of what we have read in an ancient – "that kind of double delight" we have in looking at "the children of a beautiful couple, where the eye is not more charmed with the symmetry of the parts than the mind by observing the resemblance." "In all the common subjects of poetry," the aging William Walsh told his young pupil, Pope, "the thoughts are so obvious . . . that whoever writes last must write things like what have been said before."

What strikes us most about such remarks, of which a sizable anthology could be made, is not the bravado that the post-Romantic world has been so eager to attribute to neoclassic "Augustan optimism" but rather the resignation. True, it was a resignation usually courageous, occasionally cheerful (everyone was in the same boat), at all times clear-headed and unillusioned; but in this one way, if in no other, there was something close to despair. Argue as one might that "originality" and "invention" can continue to be possible only in areas like the sciences, where new data are constantly accumulating, and that what is wanted in the arts is something else entirely (the faithful, vivid, strong presentation of life and experience), the thought of what poetry had been able to do in the greatest periods of the past, especially classical antiquity, continued to rebuke the present. Had not Boileau himself, at the end of the *Art Poétique*, raised the question: Where, given all our present achievements, is there another Virgil to pick up, subsume, and express the age? Of course the English could remind themselves that Virgil himself was not an "original." He had Homer before him. Yet if he lacked freshness, Virgil still had epic range.

Where indeed were the Virgils or where was even the promise of one? What was the difficulty? It was not as though this were a benighted age. It was a period that had every right to be proud of itself. It was, in its way, quite as good as Rome – in many ways quite superior, as even the most casual acquaintance with Roman social history would verify. Moreover, Rome had its own problems in the arts, and Virgil could hardly be called typical. Still he was there. In some way the ground was slipping beneath one's feet. One was not in the position one had expected to be. Take, as an example, that word *elegance*, so important in the whole conception of the "Second Temple." It was a good word at the start, richly sustained by all that one associated with its Latin origin and its probable cognates: *lex*, or law, and the words connected with "propriety" and "relevance" ("col*lect*," "se*lect*," and the like), as well as those that had to do with reading (*lego*), learning, study. The whole conception of *elegance* was of something won from and by means of law, form, learning: in short, "beauty with propriety," as Johnson was to define it in the *Dictionary*. Yet it had also come to mean what Johnson was to add with no thought of contradiction but only as supplement: "Beauty *without grandeur*." What had been happening to the word itself was, in miniature, the essence of what had been happening generally. Are "propriety" and "grandeur" inevitably at odds? They surely were not at odds in the great classical models themselves – not at all in what we say we admire most. Does our present feeling that they are at odds, at least for ourselves, have something to do with our own self-consciousness? In any case, there is no justification for ending in a situation where we are defensively fighting shy of "grandeur," as though it were something approaching mortal sin. (The same feeling was occasionally shared in reaction to the formalistic, anti-Victorian movement of the period from 1920 to 1960, though there was less courage in expressing it.) And in music, see what could be done: if anything justified the word "sublime" it was the work being turned out so prolifically by Handel – a Milton, a veritable Samson among composers. Why should the situation be so different in poetry? Models were available there as in nothing else, except perhaps in some areas of the visual arts.

Was there a built-in dichotomy in having embraced so warmly the classical ideal for the purposes of "propriety," "form," "refinement," and at the same time cherishing in advance (having now made the conscience captive to it) whatever the classical ideal might continue to unfold? Was the classical so completely a different world from our own that, once we went beyond the external and formal brilliance of its models, we then discovered something that no longer really applied? Not at all if we are concerned with any ideal of what art *can* be. For what we discover is something that we do not have and is wholly admirable. And what, in any case, is the alternative? To throw aside the classical legacy? No one could erase it, at least while the books exist. (Within a few years the thought was to cross more than one mind that the burning of the Alexandrian library had its advantages.) And who would seriously want to erase such an inheritance? No, it was something that had to be lived with, and as intelligently as one could. The fatigue to the spirit was that the kind of thing expected, from the challenge of the sanctified past, appeared so completely beyond one's grasp. Study, hard work, good intention did not seem to serve. One thinks of Sir Richard Blackmore, author of so many epics from *Prince Arthur* and *Alfred* to *The Nature of Man* and even *The Creation*. His discourse on "Epic Poetry" (1716) reveals how conscientiously, from the start, he had put before himself the highest ideals: sincerity, sublimity, national and cultural range, amplitude of characters, refinement in language and versification (but not too much, lest it "enervate expression" — as he feared "refinement" was tending now to do), firmness of action and plot, probability, strength and yet easy familiarity and openness of idiom. Oppressed with the burden of such high and apparently diverse ideals, Blackmore staggered under the weight, but bravely wrote on. The result was the concentrated self-intimidation in conflict with step-by-step determination parodied in Pope's couplet:

> Lest stiff, and stately, void of fire or force,
> You limp, like Blackmore, on a Lord Mayor's horse.

But while laughing at the Blackmores and their methodical attempts to combine everything that was most prized, could we not say that — in theory — this is exactly what we should be, and often are, advocating: high ideals, hard work, study and method, courage? Johnson, years later, felt that Blackmore should be viewed with some tenderness.

Worst of all for the practicing poet, the qualities now felt as most missing, in comparison with the classical achievement, increasingly began to bring back to the English mind its own creative past, especially Shakespeare and Milton. In short, the poet was now becoming flanked, in his own effort, on both sides — the parental as well as the classical-ancestral. At the same time, in a deeply disturbing way, the features of the dead parent (more removed now and therefore most susceptible to the reverential and idealizing imagination) seemed to be settling into a countenance more like that of the ancestor. Almost — to the mid-eighteenth-century poet — the parental and ancestral seemed to be linking arms as twin deities looming above him.

And was this not — as they looked back on the situation — something that had been felt, indeed half-acknowledged, from the start? Dryden, however self-confident, bland, negligent (in the best sense of the word), could speak enviously of Shakespeare as one would of the Ancients: "All the images of Nature were *still present* to him." So with Pope. He could say that "Nature and Homer were . . . the same." But though contemplating a blank-verse epic on a legendary hero, what he himself did was to translate Homer. (This was all very well, and one could certainly profit from a modernized version of Homer, though objections were inevitably raised to the use of the contemporaneous style for this purpose). But was it solely because Homer had already pre-empted every possibility of originality? Pope himself had said that "if ever there was any author who deserved the name of an *Original,* it was Shakespeare. Homer himself drew not his art so immediately from the fountains of Nature." Pope was also completely aware of something else. He, a modern poet, brought out an edition of Shakespeare. On the other hand, Shakespeare had not brought out — and would not have brought out — an edition of Chaucer or of any other writer.

Yes, by the very standard to which Pope himself adhered, he had settled in his own writing for the more specialized qualities of "refinement" and "correctness." This at least, for the English poet, remained as "one way left of excelling." But whatever Pope's individual success (and this itself quickly created a further problem for still later poets) the classical ideal of generality, of scope in subject and breadth of appeal, continued to bring back the question: What has happened to the "greater genres" — to epic and dramatic tragedy? That question, and all it implies, was to disturb the English poet henceforth, as it already disturbed a poet like William Collins, who, in his lines (1743) on Sir Thomas Hanmer's edition of Shakespeare, protests that poetry is the great exception to the pattern of progress through mere accumulative effort:

> Toil builds on Toil, and Age on Age improves.
> The Muse *alone* unequal dealt her Rage,
> And grac'd with noblest pomp her earliest Stage.

—7—

By the middle of the eighteenth century, there was an almost universal suspicion that something had gone wrong in the neoclassic adventure, whatever its success in other ways. And nothing could be more historically short-sighted and parochial than to associate this, as has so often been done, with merely a budding Romanticism restive against "neoclassic restriction." The uneasiness went far deeper, and afflicted those who strongly sympathized with the stylistic mode (or modes) of neoclassic poetry and art. This is especially true by the second half of the century. Who are the conservatives who leap to mind? They are men like Edmund Burke, who hungered for amplitude and the "sublime," or the classically minded Reynolds, who found himself, as he grew older, thinking of Michelangelo and longing for the scope and power associated with the lost "sublime." Among conservatives in poetry we think of Johnson and Goldsmith. Yet there is that illuminating moment when Boswell tells Johnson of a dispute between the Augustan-minded Goldsmith and Robert Dodsley the publisher. Goldsmith had maintained that there was no

> poetry produced in this age. Dodsley appealed to his own Collection, and maintained, that though you could not find a palace like Dryden's "Ode on St. Cecilia's Day," you had villages composed of very pretty houses; and he mentioned particularly "The Spleen." JOHNSON. "I think Dodsley gave up the question. He and Goldsmith said the same thing; only he said it in a softer manner than Goldsmith did; for he acknowledged that there was no poetry, nothing that towered above the common mark."

Essentially these conservatives are thinking and reacting in the vein typified by Sir William Temple, two or three generations before: that of an intelligent and well-read mind brought up on the classics, who is looking for the exemplification of broad classical values in the literature of his own day. (To say this is not to deny that Temple also said some silly things. It is easy to pick holes in what he says about literature; but we, as historians, have the accumulated labors of two and a half centuries of criticism and scholarship to permit us our superiority.)

Even in France, though there the neoclassic effort could be more firmly identified with their own past (as it could not with Elizabethan and Jacobean England), those who most appreciated the gains of the French Enlightenment made one great exception as the eighteenth century reached its midpoint – the arts, especially poetry. "We cannot," said Voltaire, "hold that the great feelings, the great tragic passions [in epic or drama] are able to vary indefinitely. Everything has its limits." Here we should remember that we are citing a man whose principal theme is the development of humanity through intelligence, and who, in every area in which the possibility of this occurs, is a rational optimist – clear-headed, cynical, open, courageous, confident that in almost every other way, provided mankind keeps its balance and uses its potential intelligence, humanity can transform itself for the better. Yet in the arts, he thought, and in "all those areas in which the subjects are not ceaselessly renewed, as in history or in the physical science," the door is closing; and we shall soon be left with two alternatives – routine imitation or "senseless eccentricity." As with Voltaire, so even with such a confident champion of progress as Condillac: whatever man's hopes for progress in other ways, there is one major exception, painful to admit – the inevitable "exhaustion of the arts" and the obvious decline of "imaginative strength" that is already under way.

In short, the deepening anxiety about the arts, and particularly poetry, is far from being a by-product of a general philosophy of "decline." Those who feel it most acutely are those who most prize the more general possibilities in the period in which they live, are confident, analytic, comparatively without prejudice — at least serious prejudice — and relatively immune to the hypnotic effects of nostalgia on judgment. Not that the treacheries of nostalgia were not actively present at the time. The fatigue and depression that so often seem to accompany success, in an individual or a society (we have certainly seen it reappearing now in the latter half of the twentieth century), threw a powerful bar-sinister across the optimism of the middle eighteenth century. The primitivism (Marie Antoinette playing the shepherdess),* the cult of the "noble savage," medievalism as a dream of escape from drab complexity into color and vigor, the yearning for simplicity, rural life, the spontaneity and innocence of the child: all this was there, of course; and I certainly do not wish to minimize it. In fact I think it one of the most fascinating things about the middle and latter part of the eighteenth century — one of the ways in which it is so much like our own period, and indeed more like our own than any other generation of the past five hundred years. (Another way in which it is like our own generation is that its greatest literature is possibly in its intellectual, thoughtful prose.) But the point to be emphasized is that this could happen to the degree that it did only because those at the forefront of the literary world were themselves undergoing the crisis of reconsideration we have mentioned.

* It is amusing that the Earl of Chesterfield himself was a patron of Henry Jones, "The Poetical Bricklayer," who — with Mary Collier, "The Poetical Washerwoman," and Stephen Duck, "The Thresher Poet" — is among the first of those "unspoiled geniuses" we find admired and cultivated down through Anne Yearsley, "The Poetical Milk-Woman of Bristol," to the great figure of Burns and, somewhat later, John Clare (though by the 1780's the patronage had begun to wane as the talent increased).

—8—

Whatever else can be said of the spate of critical writing that suddenly begins in the middle of the eighteenth century in England, we can describe it as an attempt, however confused at first, to reground the entire thinking about poetry in the light of one overwhelming fact: the obviously superior originality, and the at least apparently greater immediacy and universality of subject and appeal, of the poetry of earlier periods. The regrounding brought with it the fear — more openly expressed than ever before in history — that literature and the other arts as well were threatened with inevitable decline.* Nor is the matter disposed of by saying that progress is a "romantic" idea and that thoughts of the Golden Age or of historical cycles are natural to a neoclassical period. Least of all do we show much insight when we mutter that this apprehension is an old one and cite once again the sixteenth- and seventeenth-century writers who dwell on the "decay of nature." The sort of anxiety of which we are now speaking is very different from the idea of the "decay of nature." In fact, the people who felt it most strongly were, as we said, those who believed most in progress in other ways — for whom any decline in the arts was the unfortunate by-product of the increase in knowledge, communication, taste, and general civilization. And in any case we should remember that the practicing writer is quite capable of falling into apprehensions without the aid of the philosopher — especially when the cards appear to be stacked against him. This has been possible for a very long time. I refer again to that epigram left by an Egyptian writer of 2000 B.C.: "Would I had phrases that are not known . . . in new language that has not been used . . . not an utterance which has grown stale."

* See the article of John D. Scheffer, "The Idea of Decline in Literature and the Fine Arts in Eighteenth-Century England," *Modern Philology*, XXXIV (1936–37), 155–178.

Several diagnoses were advanced, many of them dovetailing with the discussion of other matters. In one approach after another, they anticipate and explore almost every approach we ourselves continue to use, two centuries later, in our own attempts to explain or rationalize the relation of present to past in the arts. There were, to begin with, the outright primitivists (so often discussed apart from this pressing, personal concern on the part of the writer). Earlier, more primitive folk, as Thomas Blackwell said in his *Enquiry into the Life and Writings of Homer* (1735), "lived naturally": their passions were simple, direct, and intense; their conversation did not consist of "the Prattle, and little pretty Forms that enervate a polished Speech" in the later periods of a culture. This approach continues without interruption and with increasing sophistication until it culminates in Wordsworth's great preface to the *Lyrical Ballads* at the end of the century. It can be hopeful (as it is in Wordsworth) – assuming that we are free, if we want, to get back to the "essential passions." But more often it assumes that the door is closed. Blackwell's remarkable book – praised by Gibbon as "an effort of genius" – is in this respect typical. What are the conditions that produce or for that matter even permit the great epics to which we look back with such admiration? The "very nerve of the Epic Strain" is the "Marvellous and Wonderful . . . But what marvellous things happen in a *well-ordered* State?" If we have the good fortune to live in a really civilized society, our lives consist of occupations and recreations – and involve a constant encounter with details and formalities – that can hardly be called "heroic"; and any hyperbolic language about this is possible only in mock-heroic or parody.

Hence if the modern poet seriously tries to achieve the "higher strain" of poetry, in anything like the traditional epic sense, he is forced to shed and put at a distance "our daily way of life: to forget the manner of sleeping, eating, and diversions. We are obliged to adopt a set of more *natural* manners, which however are foreign to us, and must be like plants raised up in hot-beds or green-houses." Now of course there are other things that can be done (Blackwell stresses the potentialities for landscape and scenic poetry — for what the nineteenth century was to call "nature poetry"). But the general level will inevitably be different. There will not be the same union of the sense of popular urgency, of the panoramic treatment of human characters, of elevation and bold confidence of style. The truth is that "a people's felicity clips the wings of their verse," and it does not seem to be given to one and the same people "to be thoroughly civilized and afford proper subjects for poetry," or at least poetry of the boldest and highest kind. And Blackwell is only half puckish when he expresses the hope, with which he is sure we shall all agree if we start to reflect, that "we [and our society] may never be a Proper Subject of an Heroic Poem."

Throughout the next forty years (1735–1775) what Blackwell is saying is repeated, developed, and — almost — taken for granted, often in the spirit of Edwin Arlington Robinson's "Miniver Cheevy," but sometimes thoughtfully. A good example of the latter is William Duff's *Essay of Original Genius* (1767), the concluding chapter of which bears the long title (here abbreviated), "That Original Poetic Genius Will in General Be Displayed in Its Ultimate Vigour in the Early . . . Periods of Society . . . and That It Will Seldom Appear in a Very Great Degree in Cultivated Life."

—9—

Meanwhile more specific diagnoses focused on the growing specialism of both the arts generally and language in particular. Typical of the former is John Brown's *Disser-*

tation on the Rise, Union, and Power, the Progressions, Separations, and Corruptions of Poetry and Music (1763), which in many ways anticipates Nietzsche and Wagner a century later. Brown begins with a comprehensive survey of primitive and semiprimitive life. In every case, the arts, especially poetry, are an intrinsic part of tribal or national life and acquire a high prestige because of this. Poetry, song, and dance are united not only with each other but with governmental legislation and the priesthood. The close interconnection of laws, oracles, poetry, music, and public ceremony provides the fertile soil from which, in a still more advanced society, the greater forms of poetry rapidly and firmly emerge – epic, building on "a kind of fabulous history," and other major forms developing afterwards. But, as the branches from the trunk of a tree continue to divide further into progressively smaller branches, the specialism of genres begins, ending finally in the short occasional poem, didactic verse, or satire. Attempts to overcome the situation are inevitably artificial. Opera, for example, in its hope to reunite poetry and music, is being developed now long after a time when "the general state of manners in Europe" would "naturally produce it."

Now that the critical intelligence of the eighteenth century was alert to the problem, the tendency of the arts to divide and specialize was quickly seen to apply to language itself. What produced that brilliantly bold use of metaphoric language that we so much admire in earlier writing? Plainly it rose from poverty of vocabulary and, in the eagerness to communicate, the use of one thing, symbolically or metaphorically, for another. When we look at our own language, are not all our abstractions a refinement upon what was originally metaphor? Our word "wrong" meant something "wrung" or twisted, and "abstraction" something "pulled away from." "Consider" meant to "con" or study the stars; "sublime" a rising up from beneath the threshold; "experience" something won from risk or danger (*ex periculo*), through the Greek *peira* (peril or risk) a cognate of "pirate." Our very words "human" and "humanity," and all the words that have developed from them, come from the word meaning "earth" (*humus*).

It is because of this situation more than anything else, said Adam Ferguson in his *History of Civil Society* (1767) — one of the pioneering works in historical sociology — that primitive man, in however rudimentary a way, is "a poet by nature" and forced by the scantiness of denotative vocabulary into a "daring freedom" of image and metaphor. The central theme of Adam Smith's *Considerations Concerning the First Formation of Languages* (1767), published the same year as Ferguson's book, is the progressive, in fact inevitable development of language from the concrete to the abstract. What Smith is saying here, though it had been suggested for years, was henceforth accepted as a basic premise. (It is typical of the century that a man who did so many other things should be so interested in this problem.) Few of the rhetorics and general studies of language, during the later eighteenth century, failed to note that metaphor and with it poetic "suggestiveness" in general are gradually lost as a language becomes more exact and denotative through use and through the growth of more analytic writing. Before long everyone was agreeing. When a small discussion group was founded in Manchester (The Literary and Philosophical Society of Manchester), one of the papers in their first volume (1781–1783) could stress that a language is naturally more poetic in its earlier stages, that, as a result, poetic feeling later becomes "minced into finer portions," and that therefore a "strong poetic character may be expected to decline, as Taste improves."

—10—

There were other diagnoses. One that is still occasionally invoked was the unique susceptibility of classical mythology to poetic treatment, as contrasted with the Christian religion. We cannot play with the truths of the Christian religion with the same inventive spontaneity. They are fixed, and we either believe them or not. But then one stopped to reflect on Dante and the major Renaissance poets, or on the sculpture and painting of the Renaissance, and the argument began to seem less forceful. And what of the Bible? There was certainly belief there. And was not the Bible at the same time one of the supreme examples of literary expression? Others thought an explanation could be found in an increase in the size of the audience that the artist now confronts. In earlier periods he was speaking directly to a small communal group. Now that his audience is larger, an inevitable mediocrity of taste begins to pervade the atmosphere in and through which he must work. (The point was raised again with the growth of mass media in the 1920's and 1930's, and is now one of our stock assumptions.) But this too, as an answer, did not ring convincingly. In fact, is it not that very generality of appeal and broad cultural involvement of which we are now deploring the lack? Such things may enter into the picture, but they are not the essential explanation. For them, as for a dozen others, one could counter every example used in argument by another that would immediately undercut it.

No, there was obviously more to the situation. Perhaps, of those mentioned, the primitivistic answer came the nearest to having some justification—at least when supplemented by what was being said about language and the growing separation of the arts. But even that had to be qualified. For example, was it really true, as Blackwell,

William Duff, and so many others were saying, that "original poetic genius" is at its most vigorous in the earliest periods of a society? Is it not rather in the *second* major period of a culture that we get this flowering in poetry and the related arts – a "golden" after a primitive or "iron" age? The time most fertile for poetry, said Richard Hurd, in his work significantly titled *The Golden Age of Queen Elizabeth* (1759), lies "somewhere between the rude essays" of a primitive period "and the refinements of reason and science." Everything most helpful or relevant to the production of the greatest poetry, said James Beattie three years later (1762), seems to converge at that point when "men are raised above savage life, and considerably improved by arts, but not advanced so high in the ascent toward politeness as to have acquired the habit of disguising their thoughts and passions, and of reducing their behaviour to the uniformity of the mode." So others continued to say throughout the 1760's and 1770's until it had become something close to orthodoxy by the time Thomas Warton published his *History of English Poetry* (1774–1781) and described the Age of Elizabeth as "the golden age of poetry" – the "most poetical" age in the history of English letters. It was with this premise, provided them by the mid-eighteenth-century reconsideration of itself, that the major English Romantics were to grow up, in their formative years, and to begin their own writing.

—11—

Still others, in searching for an explanation, found it in the self-consciousness and timidity created by the growth of criticism – a growth considered inevitable as a culture grows older, and part of the price paid for the spread of literacy. Whatever its value in other ways, it could certainly be expected to make life more difficult for the artist. This had been said, in one way or another, since the time of Sir William Temple, in the 1690's, and not only in England but even in France. But by the 1750's (the decade that is to usher in the most continually fertile period in English criticism – a period of about seventy years), the thought rapidly spreads, not as the sole or even principal answer to what has happened but as one of the important complexities that any honest consideration of the new literature must include. This may help to explain why the critical writing of these seventy years is as good as it is, and why it so rarely lost its hold on essentials or became, as an independent growth, a vine strangling the tree.

Typical of the uneasiness is the remark in Joseph Warton's *Essay on Pope* (1756) – significant because even Johnson thought it an idea that "deserves great attention": "In no polished nation, after criticism has been much studied, and the rules of writing established, has any very extraordinary work ever appeared." This is a central point in Goldsmith's *Enquiry into the Present State of Polite Learning* (1759), and Goldsmith did much to popularize it. We find the speculation of particular interest now, when one of the most striking aspects of modern literature, as Lionel Trilling says, is its susceptiblity "to being made an academic subject," and when – despite at least a hundredfold increase in the bulk of criticism – one of the subjects of least concern to this vast critical output is what most encourages or permits creative fluency. But the idea, however common in the later eighteenth century, is never developed, largely because critics – who would naturally be the ones to pursue the idea – were not eager to argue against the basis of what they themselves spent their own time doing.

The special interest of this attitude appears indirectly: that is, in its underlying sense of how much *intimidation* may have to do with the writer's fluency and what he tries to attain. Edward Young, in the *Conjectures on Original*

Composition (1759), faces the whole matter of intimidation directly, though he is thinking less about the effect of criticism itself than about the intimidating pressures, on the practicing writer, of great models of the past — those great models on whom the writer has naturally been educated. Young's approach appears to be more interesting and valuable. The disappointment comes in his conclusion on what the writer should do about it. In effect Young asks that the writer pull himself up by his own bootstraps: let us imitate the *general spirit* of the past writers we admire (their boldness, their openness, their range) but keep selecting our own *means* of working toward it.

—12—

He that imitates the *Iliad*, says Young, is not imitating Homer. Of course. And what Young was saying is what Longinus himself had said sixteen centuries before in *On the Sublime.*

But even if this was true — and of course it was — how do we proceed? When we are actually confronted with specific answers, we soon complain of being suffocated or inhibited, of being denied the opportunity to contribute "creatively" and "freely" on our own; and we at once begin — usually with some success — to pick holes in what has been presented us. But as soon as we feel we have pushed all this aside, and at last stand free and ready to make our own contribution, the human heart shrinks at its new nakedness and its new gift of what Santayana calls "vacant liberty." We start once again to crave specific direction, and turn reproachfully, notebook in hand, on those who are now exhorting us — in the very spirit we had before demanded — to "go and do likewise."

The later eighteenth century did make an effort to provide helpful answers, as much as any period in the history of critical writing. Boldly and specifically it tried to concentrate, as criticism has rarely done before or since, on both the psychology of genius and the stylistic means of attaining the highest possible reach of art, the "sublime" — and without embarrassment or apology. The particular details may be open to endless quibble. But the concern and effort were to prove healthful in the highest degree. Was not the greatest of classical legacies, after all, the Greek ideal of *arete* or excellence — the "vision of greatness," in Whitehead's phrase — that had proved so fertile in ancient Greece and again in the Renaissance? But the struggle to recapture it, in the eighteenth-century wrestle with itself and with the classical ideal, was far from easy.

III | The Eighteenth-Century Reconsideration

Hume and the Essential Diagnosis

Whatever the explanation, one always seemed to come back to that disturbing question: Where are the "greater genres" – the epic and the tragic drama – or at least reasonable equivalents? For even if we were to say (as the later eighteenth century was beginning to say) that we have all been much too obsessed with genres and should be more open to other possible forms and uses of poetry, must we still not admit that poetry has been cultivating progressively smaller plots or concentrating on less general interests? And if this should be true of poetry, would it not in time prove true of any art? The question, as we have said, has haunted every English poet since Milton, however much he may have resisted it.

Take just four instances, purposely selected because each writer is so vigorous and independent. Johnson, loathing any cant about "decline" or about anything else that reflected on man's freedom – Johnson who was "always angry," as he said, "whenever he heard earlier periods extolled at the expense of the modern" – could still permit Imlac in *Rasselas* (chapter X) to say that, whatever the nation and language and however different the explanations offered, "it is commonly observed that the early writers are in possession of nature, and their followers of art: that the first excel in strength and invention, and the latter in elegance and refinement." Again, Keats could compare the ancients and the Elizabethans to "Emperors of vast Provinces," while by contrast "each of the moderns like an Elector of Hanover governs his petty state, and knows how many straws are swept from the causeways . . . and has a continual itching that all the housewives should have their coppers well scoured." Or think of Emerson, so free of timidity before the past, who still could say of Milton that he served as the great "stair or high table-land to let down the English genius from the summit of Shakespeare." And, to glance ahead to the twentieth century, there are those lines of Yeats:

> Shakespearean fish swam the sea, far away from land;
> Romantic fish swam in nets coming to the hand;
> What are all those fish that lie gasping on the strand? *

—2—

If poetry in its earlier periods was "more vigorous than it is in its modern state," as Hugh Blair said – in those *Lectures on Rhetoric and Belles-Lettres* (1783) that were to be used in universities as a textbook for the next half-century – it is because poetry "included then the *whole burst* of the human mind, the whole exertion of its imaginative faculties." In other words poetry had a monopoly on the potentialities of both expression and subject. What so many had been saying not only about the increasing subdivision in the arts generally but also about language in particular (its growing specialism into denotative abstraction) applied only too obviously to the human mind itself. The same remorseless tendency to separation – indeed compartmentalization – takes place *psychologically* through the specialism, crowding, and competition that seem inevitable in an increasingly civilized or – if the word is more accurate – increasingly "organized" society. An age of the major poetry and the arts generally, said Goldsmith, is followed by that of "philosophy" and increasingly analytic thinking. After this will come the age of the commentator, glossing and refining upon the previous "analytic" age. With the division and specialism that results – as even Bacon, the father of modern specialism, predicted – "universality" is lost.

Hence the question seriously presents itself: Would a man with the general mental and imaginative endowment

* "Three Great Movements," reprinted with permission of The Macmillan Company from *The Collected Poems of W. B. Yeats*, copyright 1933 by The Macmillan Company, renewed 1961 by Bertha Georgie Yeats; also with permission of Mr. M. B. Yeats and Macmillan and Company, London.

of a Homer, a Dante, a Shakespeare, now be writing poetry at all? Or, if he did, would he not be writing a kind of poetry that would exploit only a fraction of his potential range of talent? If there are mute Shakespeares and Miltons who are not writing works even remotely comparable to those of Shakespeare and Milton, then what is the explanation? One of the few premises of the eighteenth century about which there was little or no disagreement (and it is hard to quarrel with it now) is that the amount of *potential* talent or genius is always much the same in proportion to the population generally.

Is poetry, in other words, condemned to be only an initial and intermediary experience for a culture? To put it bluntly, as Peacock was later to do in the *Four Ages of Poetry* (1820):

> Poetry was the mental rattle that awakened the attention of intellect in the infancy of civil society; but for the maturity of mind to make a serious business of the playthings of its childhood is as absurd as for a full-grown man to rub his gums with coral, and cry to be charmed to sleep by the jingle of silver bells.

And Peacock presents, with distilled irony, the helplessness of the modern world if it really wants to write a poetry comparable to that of the envied past. After a primitive or "Iron" age comes a "Golden" age (the great days of Greece, in the ancient world, or, in the modern, the age of Shakespeare and the Renaissance). Then a "Silver Age" takes over – Rome, in classical antiquity, or neoclassic "Augustan" England (Milton, in the seventeenth century, is a sort of cross between "Gold" and "Silver"). And what is now about to appear is an Age of Brass.

Granted that Peacock was intentionally overstating the situation. He was at least half-teasing his friend Shelley, who then nobly responded in the *Defence of Poetry*. But could it be true – however unwilling we are to admit the thought — that poetry as a major experience of man is, by definition, a quasi-primitive, or to put it more accurately a *postprimitive* achievement of a culture? — indispensable for human development, and capable at its highest moments of coalescing diversity of experience into a unity of expression that nothing else could have done or is likely to do again, but nonetheless past? The central premise of Macaulay's famous essay on Milton (1825) is that "as civilization advances, poetry almost necessarily declines." To dismiss the essay as a quaint aberration of mind indicating how little Macaulay could have cared for poetry (he knew *Paradise Lost* by heart as well as many other major poems scarcely read by his twentieth-century detractors) is wildly, indeed ludicrously far from the mark. In every point that Macaulay discusses — the growing abstraction and denotative exactness of language, the contrast between the creative arts and the cumulative sciences, the dispelling of imaginative readiness in belief and the sense of wonder through the increasingly specialized habits (and resultant cautions and skepticism) of analysis — he is drawing on almost a full century of painful reconsideration and self-debate. He was entirely justified in referring to "that most orthodox article of literary faith, that the earliest poets are the best." In fact that old Bohemian, Walter Savage Landor, was to put it far more abruptly: a rib of Shakespeare would have made a Milton; a rib of Milton all poets since.

Was poetry therefore only a glorious survival? Was it — and this was a question that Romanticism was to face from the start, that it was forced to live with during its most creative period, and that we are now facing once again (indeed now more than ever) — was it like those great animals we find in the prairies and jungles of Africa and parts of the Americas, still able for a while to roam and graze freely, but inevitably doomed by the remorseless spread of organized life that we call civilization?

If so, should we not intelligently and realistically accept the fact that this particular stage of Western man is over? Is there not already, as Joseph Priestley said, more than enough poetry from the past to occupy the mind and to help serve in its education? How many people are there – he asks with common sense – who have both the leisure and a strong inclination "to read, much less to read with *care*, or to *study*, all that is really excellent" from the past? The question was by no means so Philistine as our stock responses might lead us to suppose. Priestley was no fool. One of the most inventive and original minds of the century (historian, sociologist, theologian, psychologist, the discoverer of oxygen, and a perceptive critic of literature), he could sympathetically view the arts, as did Bacon before him, in the light of the general human endeavor. Were the arts something special or were they not? Was there something in the very nature of the arts (the inevitable by-product of their value, their necessity) that suddenly thwarted them as they reached a certain point in their development? Priestley thought that there was. It was a cruel paradox for one who believed in the possibilities of progress if we only used our minds. But it was a paradox created by the incorrigible nature of man.

—3—

Yet assuming there was a point, perhaps more than a point, to the apprehensions about what had been happening to poetry (and what, by implication, could in time happen to the other arts if it had not begun to do so already), how convincing were the explanations? Or perhaps we should put it in the singular: how convincing was the explanation? For the shared assumption was that great poetry – poetry central to the general experience of man, prodigal in its range of imagination, hospitable to every interest, vigorous, and unapologetically, immediately bold

– is culturally determined by circumstances possible only in some less "advanced" age, whether because of the more "natural" environment of human life, the more concrete, less developed state of the language, or the less regulated character of society and of the human mind.

The explanations, however seductive, quickly generated counterarguments, often in the same writer, and throughout the second half of the eighteenth century we find a more searching reconsideration of the whole question of the arts in relation to their own past. The picture is one of many-sided and continuing debate, in which the burden of the past was affirmed, denied or qualified. Was what we say we so admire in the great poetry and art of the past really the product of unique circumstances of life, or are we merely indulging in a loose form of epiphenomenalism – noting several things that occurred at the same time, connecting them, and saying that one produces, or at least helps to produce, the other? Any such question naturally conflicted with the new historical sophistication of the eighteenth century, its justifiable pride that it was getting away from traditional chronicle-history and was creating a new appreciation of the "organic," the interconnected – of history "in the round." Again, were the achievements of the past – or, to put it more fairly, of any one particular *part* of the past similar in length of time (a mere half-century, at most a century) to what we decide to call the "present" – really so impressive as was claimed? Even if we become very selective, are what we call the "greater genres" really greater in every respect? And concentrating even more selectively, taking only the isolated peaks of achievement to which we pay such lip-service: are they *really* what we want at the present time? Or is it only something analogous that we want?

Finally why, in our dissatisfactions, do we so strongly clutch at deterministic explanations that relieve us from the burden of deciding not only what we most want but also what we can and should do about it? Could this not be the real "burden" after all — not determinism, but the burden of choice?

—4—

For of course the primitivistic diagnosis (so also with the idealization of other periods — "second," "golden" or whatever) was wide open to all the charges of foreshortening and selectivity that can be made against any form of nostalgia. The power of nostalgia to distort judgment is endemic in us all, and our confidence that we are free of its prejudices and defenses is never justified. While we may be quick to note what it can do to the opinions of others, we ourselves, in thinking of our own lives or something larger, are always weighing the vulnerable, unsatisfying present against a richer, more vivid past (or future, if we are still young enough) — richer and more vivid because we select only the highest possible moments and then coalesce them into a more condensed unity than any actual experience could ever provide. So few of our moments, as Johnson said, are "filled up with objects adequate to the mind of man" that the "hunger of imagination" that "preys incessantly upon life" is always seeking something else either to fatten and fill out the present moment in order to make it more tolerable or pleasant, or else to serve as contrast. Hence our susceptibility to "envy" (the imagined state of another) or to thoughts of the past and future, so much more "pliant and ductile" to the imagination than the stubborn present with its unwelcome burden and complication of detail: "The truth is that no mind is much employed upon the present: recollection and anticipation fill up almost all our moments." The most powerful treatment of the treachery of imaginative nostalgia in the whole of literature is provided by Johnson, so much at the center of this period (it is indeed the essence of his moral writings): powerful because it rises so completely, in everything he touches, from shared experience, and, while tender and brooding, making every possible excuse, it simultaneously — to use Reynolds' remark about him — clears the mind of a great deal of rubbish.

The more sophisticated could easily laugh at Joseph Warton's idealization of a primitive past in his youthful poem *The Enthusiast* (1744), where he spoke of the health and joy of primitive lovers ("who in sheltering groves / Warm caves, and deep-sunk vallies liv'd and lov'd"), eating berries and acorns, and clasping each other "Unaw'd by shame beneath the beechen shade." So with the authoress of the popular *Compleat Housewife* (1736), a Mrs. Smith, who, in providing elaborate recipes for cooking, felt it necessary to apologize and refer nostalgically to "the Infant Age of the World," when "Mankind stood in no need of additional Sauces, Ragoos, Etc., to produce a good appetite" (healthy constitutions, wholesome air and exercise, and "exemption from anxious cares" made our modern elaboration of cookery unnecessary). And when General Paoli, says Boswell, remarked that "in a state of nature a man and woman uniting together would form a strong and constant affection," and that "the same causes of dissension would not arise between them as occur between husband and wife in a civilized state," everyone could relish Johnson's reply: "They would have dissensions enough, though of another kind. One would choose to go a hunting in this wood, the other in that . . ." True, long-drawn-out bickering would be unlikely. It would be only too easy to leave or dispose of an unwanted mate.

But was there not the same radical selectivity of bright moments, qualities, and expressions in the imaginations of those who — quick to laugh at the sort of thing just mentioned — turn to the past with more studied veneration and analysis, weighing the repeatedly sifted residue against the disorder and slow crawl of the present? Confront them, as their principal poetic diet for a mere decade, with the Elizabethan poetic miscellanies of any one decade and note whether the concentrated admiration of the period qua period remains at the same level of intensity. Put them down next to the Southwark brothels adjoining the Elizabethan theaters and have them push their way, for only a couple of years, to performances of the *average* Elizabethan play: would the sharpened critical delight that they have in *Hamlet* or *Macbeth* continue to be extended so generously to the period as a whole? Would they still retain that tender openness — that condescending eagerness to be pleased at everything that proves the now-lost "health" and "unity" of society ("the *whole burst* of mind") — as the crowds rushed past them, in reverse direction, to attend the latest execution at Tyburn? If they shift their ground, and say that what they are thinking of is the court or at least the more sophisticated — that there at least the higher uses of the drama were appreciated as rarely before and never since — they are simply thinking of them as some of the Elizabethans had thought of the ancients. "In modern states," said Francis Bacon, the theater "is esteemed but as a toy," while "among the ancients it was used as a means of educating men's minds to virtue." And those large audiences of the past clamoring to read Homer, Virgil, and Milton — all of whom tended to be put together by the imagination in what Keats called an "immortal free-masonry" — one wondered. It seemed that it was now, in the incorrigible present of the eighteenth century, that they were coming more into their own. No one in the Roman Senate seems to have quoted Homer and Virgil to the extent that the present members of Parliament did. As for Milton, his hope had been to find "fit audience . . . though few." It was now, in this century, that he was being so widely read. As the German critic and traveler K. P. Moritz said in 1782: "The English national writers are in all hands . . . My landlady, who is only a tailor's widow, reads her Milton, and tells me that her late husband first fell in love with her on this very account, because she read Milton with such proper emphasis."

Of course all this could be put with too impatient a reductionism. But was it not justified as a temporary reply to a nostalgia itself so reductionistic in its automatic swing from the present to an imagined past at once simplified and condensed? "The age will never again return," sighed Joseph Warton in an essay for the *Adventurer* (1754), "when a Pericles, after walking with Plato in a portico built by Phidias and painted by Apelles, might repair to hear a pleading of Demosthenes or a tragedy of Sophocles." "It will never return," said Gibbon, "because it never existed . . . [Pericles] could enjoy no very great pleasure from the conversation of Plato, who was born the same year he himself died," while Apelles and Demosthenes "survived Alexander the Great, whose death is above a century posterior to that of Pericles" (*Index Expurgatorius*, No. 30).

And most of us are far guiltier in stretching the chronological limits of what from the past we sift and coalesce into ideal. As Wordsworth was to say, in an article he wrote for Coleridge's *The Friend* (1809): "There are two errors into which we easily slip when thinking of past times." One error lies in overlooking "the large overbalance of worthlessness that has been swept away," and selecting only the very best as "typical." In our imaginative voyaging through the past, we are like those travelers through the jungle who are told where the grave mounds of giants from earlier days may be found. When we find the grave, with the remains of what may indeed prove to have been a giant, we then assume that he was typical

("There were giants in those days") rather than that he had been given such a mound in the first place and then remembered simply because he happened to have been a giant. The second error is that we so quickly, in our habitual feelings, divide time merely into two parts, past and present, and then "place these in the balance . . . not considering that the present is in our estimation not more than a period of thirty years, or half a century at most, and that the past is a mighty accumulation of *many* such periods." It is precisely for these reasons that, as Ortega y Gasset was to say in our own century, every age will inevitably feel itself "empty" in comparison with the past.

—5—

No, the answer was not to be found in the nostalgic idealization of the circumstances of past periods (primitive or "second-period," "iron" or "gold," or – most attractive of all – "iron-*cum*-gold"). A little reflection will remind us that what is really distinctive or greatest about *King Lear* is not uniquely the product of the Elizabethan social ambience, and that even if we could bring back those particular circumstances a similar result would probably not occur again. As with sociolatry of period so with the idolatry of the "greater genres" in poetry or for that matter in any art. If, as Friedrich Schlegel was to say, the "epic" (meaning the conventional Homeric type of epic) is by definition a product of a postprimitive society, though only of one that had been unusually blessed, we should honestly ask whether it is this particular form of poetry that we so deeply crave in our impatience with the present. "Great models," said Edward Young, in his *Conjectures on Original Composition* (1759), which was to have so much influence on the creative courage of German writers during the next half-century, "*engross, prejudice* and *intimidate.*" And in Schiller's essay "On Naive and Sentimental Poetry"

(1795–96), where he puts the case of the moderns versus the earlier (naive) poets, he points out how easy it is to depreciate the moderns — indeed how inevitable — when we take for granted and state the criteria in exactly those terms that "constitute the highest achievement" of the earlier poets — those terms that define "their greatest originality and sublimity." Naturally the dice are loaded. But reverse the situation. "Take, in the moderns, what characterizes *them*, what makes their special merit," and the naive and earlier poets "will not be able to support the comparison any better, and Homer less than any other." The superiority of the modern, at least potentially, "relates to *ideas*" and the active interplay of real and ideal, of experience and the human mind. In the more self-conscious age in which we are living, our backward glance at more simplified eras carries with it the prejudiced bias, the condescension of delight, with which we view a child. The child, however complete and simple at that particular stage, is also being valued because we conceive him to be full of future "promise."

But remove that special context — that frame of subjective and merely "taught" association — and present us only with the work directly, as if from another hand or another period, and our condescending smile of pleasure will turn to a frown. I think here of Arthur Koestler's essay "The Anatomy of Snobbery," which is somewhat in the vein of Schiller. The point is that snobbery arises from prizing a particular context (historical or in other ways associative) rather than the intrinsic merit of a thing or person — legitimate enough except that we so often confuse the two and insist that what we are talking about is the latter when it is only the former of which we are really thinking. One of his examples is that forged group of thirteenth-century Gothic wall-paintings "discovered" at Lübeck in 1948 but actually the work of Lothar Malskat.

"A fabulous discovery of lost masterpieces," said Chancellor Adenauer, who presided at the ceremonies attended by most of the art experts of Europe. They in turn joined in praising the work as giving us the healthful confidence, the purity, the simple cleanliness and firmness so typical of the period but so impossible to find in our own. Malskat's confession to the police two years later brought contemptuous denials from the art experts who had studied and praised the work: the man, they said, wanted publicity (undeniably true). When the dust settled, and it turned out that Malskat had also manufactured scores of Rembrandts, Corots, and Watteaus (some already accepted as "original" and others in stock for future distribution), the reaction was not at all the result of the strictly "aesthetic values" on the solemn analysis of which we so pride ourselves. In fact it was based on grounds that contradict the theoretical values we usually invoke. The immediate collapse into silence was like that which took place in the student, mentioned by Northrop Frye, who subscribed to the belief that "purity" in art had disappeared since the disruption of the unity and simplicity of the Medieval and Renaissance world, and who had little use in particular for the nineteenth century (a period blowsy, divided, and, above all, too near – far too much about it was known). The student's enthusiasm for the Christmas carol "Good King Wenceslaus," hitherto praised by him as "early" and "fresh," completely evaporated on learning that the words were a nineteenth-century poem. Like Francis Jeffrey in 1810, most of us have speculated about the reception (critical as well as popular) that would be given to a Shakespearean play, like *The Tempest*, if the author were not already known beforehand – if it were assumed, in fact, that the play was a modern one (obvious archaisms in language would of course be eliminated – but it is not they we presumably cherish). But if we confess the speculation to others, it is with an uneasy smile and little more. To pursue it with a shrewd and honest imagination would involve a more drastic questioning of ourselves — of our stock responses, of our confidence in our ability to respond immediately, without the help and security of a given context, to what we all say we most deeply value — than most of us care to indulge.

—6—

There is, in short, *prejudice,* as Young had said — prejudice in the literal sense of pre-judgment, driven in upon us so early and so constantly reinforced as to become habitual. Take a single example. Those epics (selectively picked and taught us with such admiration): do not even the best have long stretches that fail to delight us — to *fill* the mind and the imagination to the extent that the very greatest poetry is expected to do? Inevitably, it could be answered: we cannot expect to remain at every moment at the highest pitch of intensity. This is true. But are we likely to show the same indulgence — the same eagerness to be pleased by long versified intervals — to a modern epic dealing with parliamentary affairs or some other large public issue? That the mere posing of the question could seem absurd to so many people — like G. H. Lewes' later question whether a modern blank-verse tragedy would have a change if the hero's name were Wiggins — illustrates the extent to which we can be insidiously prejudiced by association, by the patina of the past. We will forgive those less-than-intense stretches in Homer, Virgil, or Milton — even love and admire them — but for extraneous reasons. Even so, Walter Savage Landor, however much of a classicist, told the startled Crabb Robinson that "the greater part of Homer is trash," and, though he knew Italian so well, that about one-seventieth of Dante was real poetry. ("This led me," said Robinson, "to explain

Schlegel's theory of epic poetry, which Landor seemed both to comprehend and like.") Landor always spoke strongly and liked to shock. But taking this for granted, was it not true that our threshold of expectation had been constantly rising – that we were becoming far more querulous and exacting about what is "poetry" and what is not? Like the giraffe, we were now living off the top of the trees. The anthologized selections of the "best" parts of only the "best" poets were becoming our habitual diet, with that inevitable increase in fastidiousness which Johnson, himself susceptible to it, delighted to puncture ("elegance refined into impatience").

Of course. And one result was the creation throughout the later eighteenth century of something that we still very much live with – indeed live with now even more than did the Romantics and the nineteenth century generally: the concept (sternly controlling in practice however blithely denied in theory) of "pure poetry" – poetry distilled if necessary from relevances other than personal, aesthetic, and verbal, but in any case cherishing, and moving as much as possible toward, condensed suggestion. The essence of the argument was later put in Edgar Allan Poe's "The Poetic Principle" (1848). A long poem, said Poe, is a contradiction in terms. Those stretches of anything except powerful or magical condensations of phrase are not "poetry." They are mere filler. When I say that we continue to subscribe to this in practice if not theory (for our theory is, of course, always open to the "larger" forms – do we not still teach Homer, Dante, Shakespeare, and Milton?), I should at once emphasize that we need not be thinking of the particular kind of imagery and idiom that Poe had in mind. The two important points are that: (1) We still are thinking (or at least have until very recently been thinking) of an analogous – indeed even more drastic – condensation in the use of language, with the inevitable hurdles this creates for those large audiences that have now deserted us and to which we look back with envy when we speak of the preindustrial past ("iron," "gold," or even Augustan "silver"). (2) The substratum of feeling remains, indeed has increased, that what makes up the daily interests and experiences of modern man – aside from the inner life – is outside the permissible, respectable possibilities of poetry, except for attack or regret, with the further inhibition or complication that what the Romantics prized had, by the first third of the twentieth century, also become *verboten*. The "antiromantic" movement of twentieth-century formalism was far more a reaction against what we may call the flavor of the romantic idiom and a resentment of the stance (including the hard-won confidence) of the romantic poet than it was against the new, post-neoclassic selectivity in what was still considered to be "poetry" and what was not. We should perhaps use the phrase "temptations to selectivity," keeping in mind the genuine hope and effort of the major Romantics to write in the "larger" forms, especially the poet who was to be most identified throughout the next century with the concept of "pure poetry": the great "test of Invention," said Keats, is "a long poem . . . Did our great poets ever write *short* pieces?"

—7—

Yet when all such qualifications were brought to bear, fostering a juster, less prejudiced comparison of past and present works of literature, it was still impossible not to feel that something was seriously hampering the contemporary poet.

Toward the end of the century such anxieties especially focused on the drama. "At the origins of the romantic movement," as George Steiner says, "lies an explicit attempt to revitalize the major forms of tragedy. In fact, romanticism began as a critique of the failure . . . to carry on the great traditions of the Elizabethan and baroque theatre. It was in the name of drama that the romantics assailed neoclassicism." It could always be argued that the classical "epic" — the Homeric type of epic, with its legendary heroes, its use of mythology and fabulous adventure — was a special kind of thing, appropriate to a particular kind and level of society that was long since past and that indeed may never have actually existed except in Homeric Greece.* Even Keats, "cowering," as he said, "under the wing of great poets," was beginning to wonder, as he started *Hyperion,* whether epic poems were not a "splendid imposition" on the modern world. But the drama — the direct portrayal of human beings in action — was not, as either aim or result, a genre in the limited and specific sense that the classical "epic" was. It admitted unlimited variety, unlimited subtlety in character and expression. It may be impossible to write a modern epic without feeling Homer and Virgil hanging over you. But the form of the drama was potentially more open than any other. Why should not we ourselves be equally open now in our approach to it? That was what Johnson asked, in arguing that inventive originality was always possible if only we shed our superstitious reverence of the dead ("blind reverence acting upon fancy"). He was thinking especially of the drama, but also of the fictional portrayal of life in any

* Far from being a reflection on *Paradise Lost* (almost universally admired in every country of Europe), this was a tribute. With all the odds against him, and born, as he feared, in "an age too late" for the epic, Milton succeeded magnificently. Much of the admiration arises from his success in defying the apparently inevitable. But it was not to be done again because what Milton so powerfully called into aid as supplement to and difference from Homer could itself be done only once. Yet Milton's example of defiance on behalf of the heroic continued to haunt the imagination; and it is because of this as much as anything that, when the English poet got up the courage to try the heroic, he adopted the Miltonic robes and stance with the Longinian belief, often justified, that confidence and spirit are contagious.

form of writing. After mentioning the difficulties the modern writer faces in competition with the past, he goes on (*Adventurer*, No. 95) to stress "the alterations which time is always making in the modes of life." The passions of man, which keep the movement of life in progress, may be few when only simply and elementally described. But they are capable of constant variation — and more than mere variation — when considered, frankly and directly, in the constantly changing context of "the living world." The objects of love, hate, ambition, envy, loyalty, fear, will vary, and so even more the modes of expressing them:

> Avarice has worn a different form as she actuated the usurer of Rome and the stock-jobber of England; and idleness itself, how little soever inclined to the trouble of invention, has been forced from time to time to change its amusements, and contrive different methods of wearing out the day.
>
> Here then is the fund from which those who study mankind may fill their compositions with an inexhaustible variety . . .

And a writer "must be confessed to look with little attention upon scenes thus perpetually changing" who cannot catch and express them before they are made stale by repetition:

> The complaint, therefore, that all topics are pre-occupied is nothing more than the murmur of ignorance or idleness, by which some discourage others and some themselves: the mutability of mankind will always furnish writers with new images . . .

The major Romantics never lost their healthful confidence that, in or through the drama, or something like it, the open door could eventually be found. Their greatest lyric poetry (as in Keats's odes) may itself be described as an attempt to begin a new approach to drama, if not of the conventional kind. And it is at least possible that Keats, if he had lived even to the age of fifty (and therefore had five times his active career of five years still before him at his disposal), would have fulfilled the hope he mentions (1819) after writing the odes, *Lamia,* and the *Fall of Hyperion*: that a few long poems, "written in the course of the next six years . . . would nerve me up to the writing of a few fine Plays – my greatest ambition when I do feel ambitious."

But to say that the poetic drama, unlike the epic, was forever open – that it was not, like the classical epic, a special genre tied to the particular historical conditions (or rather the permissive allowances) of a less advanced period – only brought one back more directly to Shakespeare, and to the question: why are there no Shakespeares on the present horizon? Or if that is too naive a question, why at least is there nothing approaching or analogous to the Shakespearean achievement? The neoclassic reconsideration of itself, in Germany as well as England, had almost replaced the ancients with a "modern," or near-modern, hero-of-letters as an exemplar of what the modern writer could do. And one would think this an immense encouragement to the modern artist, the modern poet. As the Schlegels were to say, the way for the modern is here opened: we only have to "go and do likewise."

Why should it be so hard? Even if we can put at arm's length the seductions of historical and sociological nostalgia, and realistically reduce those past periods (as periods) to size and manageability, we are still confronted by an inhibition that, when we look into our hearts, has less to do with utopian social and linguistic circumstances than we defensively claim. Was it, after all, a case of simple psychological inhibition – an inhibition still further intensified by our own admiration of Shakespeare? Could this widespread feeling that the "advance" (or complication) of what we call civilization was unpropitious to poetry – that it seriously hampered the poet and would in time seriously hamper the artist generally — be explained more simply, and more truthfully, by psychological factors, by the universal human hope to make a genuine contribution and the fact that in the past so much had already been done so well that it seemed impossible to compete in the same way? Was the mere existence of the past beginning to exert an enormous pressure on poetry and forcing it into less promising directions?

—8—

It was David Hume, back in the middle of the century, who put the essence of the problem most clearly. In his essay "Of the Rise and Progress of the Arts and Sciences," he considers different facets of the subject and then advances his "fourth observation": that when the arts "come to perfection in any state, from that moment they naturally, or rather necessarily, decline, and seldom or never revive in that nation where they formerly flourished."

What Hume has just said is, he admits, theoretically puzzling. In fact, it is "at first sight . . . contrary to reason," since it is hard not to believe that the potential genius of mankind is much the same in any age. Yet it is an observation "conformable to experience," whether rationally convincing or not. Repeatedly we find that a cluster of genius in which an art is carried to the highest pitch is then followed by a dearth; and a long period seems to be necessary before a similar cluster of genius occurs again in the same art. A striking example is the Renaissance of the 1500's as contrasted with post-Augustan Rome — with the age, so fortunate in other respects, of the Antonines:

> The models left us by the ancients gave birth to all the arts about two hundred years ago, and have mightily advanced their progress in every country of Europe. Why had they not a like effect during the reign of Trajan and his successors,

when they were much more entire, and were still more admired and studied?

Is not the real answer that "a noble emulation is the source of every excellence"? If, in a period just before us, an art seems to have attained a "perfection," this very achievement, pressing on the artist that follows, "extinguishes emulation, and sinks the ardour of generous youth." A man's genius, at the beginning of his life, is as little known to himself as others. Only after many trials, followed by some success, does he dare to

> think himself equal to those undertakings, in which those who have succeeded have fixed the admiration of mankind. If his own nation be already possessed of many models . . . he naturally compares his own juvenile exercises with these; and, being sensible of the great disproportion, is discouraged from any further attempts, and never aims at a rivalship with those authors whom he so much admires. A noble emulation is the source of every excellence. Admiration and modesty naturally extinguish this emulation; and no one is so liable to an excess of admiration and modesty as a truly great genius.

Hume does not elaborate at the moment on what happens when emulation proves so difficult. But in his essay "Of Simplicity and Refinement" (where he states that "the *excess* of refinement is now more to be guarded against than ever") he goes a little further: after an art has reached a high level, "the endeavor to *please by novelty* leads men wide of simplicity and nature."

Meanwhile Hume adds a remark of particular interest to those who had been searching among other explanations (as we still do) for reasons why an art may flourish so brilliantly in one country and not at all in a neighboring nation with the same apparent advantages and much the same general background. It is never, he says, to the advantage of any nation "to have the arts imported from their neighbours in too great perfection. This extinguishes emulation, and sinks the ardour of generous youth. So many models of Italian painting brought to England, instead of exciting an artist, are the cause of their small production . . . The same perhaps was the case of Rome when it received the arts from Greece." Similarly, the multitude of French writings dispersed over Germany, Holland, and the Scandinavian countries during the past century and a half – 1600 to 1750 – has thus far hindered these nations, says Hume, from cultivating their own literature with confidence.

—9—

There are two points in particular made by Hume, whose uncanny perceptions in so many other ways have continued to arouse or bedevil our thinking since his time. First, he implies that decline is inevitable (and not for any Spenglerian reason – Hume is no post-Hegelian believer in the determinism of the *Zeitgeist* – but rather for empirical reasons that have to do with the way that human nature insists on behaving). But we need not linger on this matter of inevitability. Hume was no dogmatist; he could quickly change his position when given additional facts to consider. The second point is the important one: that the artist, because of the spirit of emulation – because of his need to feel that he has a chance before the accumulated "perfection of the past" – is in danger either of giving up, or else of manicuring the past, or, finally, of searching, in compensation, for novelty for its own sake.

In bringing up this directly human problem of emulation, Hume resurrects some remarks by Velleius Paterculus (I. xvii), written about the year A.D. 30: When we feel ourselves unable to excel (or even to equal) the great predecessors immediately before us, hope and emulation languish; we gradually resign the pursuit in which they have excelled and try to discover a new one:

> Genius is fostered by emulation . . . As in the beginning we are fired with the ambition to overtake those whom we regard as leaders, so, when we have despaired of being able either to surpass or even to equal them, our zeal wanes with our hope. It ceases to follow what it cannot overtake, and, abandoning the old field as pre-empted, seeks a new one.*

This is one of those instances in which an idea or attitude expressed by a long-forgotten writer becomes alive once again and is repeated in a new context because it seems to make sense. Velleius touched home to very few people before Hume; but henceforth we find him briefly quoted or echoed by many who knew or had read Hume, such as Lord Kames, Alexander Gerard, Joseph Priestley, or Archibald Alison. Not that they carry it very far. Their speculations tend to be limited and indirect, revealing a general, unlocalized suspicion that they seem unwilling to apply to literature in detail. Kames, for example, in his *Sketches of the History of Man* (1774), cites the effect of Newton on mathematics in Great Britain since Newton's day — the whole study of it has since languished. Kames also speculates about the effect on emulation of the great painters of the Italian Renaissance, and compares Raphael, Michelangelo, and Titian to large oaks that screen new plants from the "sunshine of emulation."

Yet they take for granted the implications for poetry (with which they are all more concerned) and at least touch on the idea suggested by Hume and developed somewhat more by Alison near the end of the century, that the inevitable pressure on the artist will increasingly force him to grasp at innovation for its own sake unless he quits the

* Velleius, in advancing this idea, is particularly interested in finding "the reasons why men of similar talents" seem to cluster at particular times, after which there is a drop in performance. To explain it "I can find no one answer of the truth of which we can be certain." But since it occurs in every art, regardless of place, he has finally, he says, settled on this explanation.

field entirely. In the process, the artist will be led "gradually to forget the end of his art, in his attempt to display his superiority in the art itself." In every art in the past that has attained a high level and then declined, we see "the same gradual desertion of the *end* of the art for the *display* of the art itself." This is what "decadence" is.

—10—

I suspect that one reason the psychological effect of the past on emulation was not followed up in detail is that it was seen most clearly by men who were fundamentally conservative, in the broader sense of that word: by men who valued and wished to conserve the gains in general insight (and, if you will, "progress" and "refinement") that had been won since the Middle Ages and the Renaissance. Such men – they would include Johnson, Burke, Reynolds, Goldsmith, Voltaire, Hume himself, and, in Germany, Lessing, Goethe, Schiller – were far from eager to point out that the past, by its mere existence, was complicating the efforts of present-day writers.* For they understood only too well the temptation to reject the past and to pursue novelty for its own sake, with all the attendant dangers of the merely trivial, specialized, or aberrant. They took for granted the fickleness in taste that Byron had in mind when he compared our temptation to reject past achievement and our desire to assert ourselves – if only by announcing something different – with the Athenian who voted for the exile of Aristides the Just simply

* Cf. Johnson's unguarded remark, despite his almost automatic temptation to take issue with any general proposition suddenly tossed at him: "I told him," said Boswell (14 April 1775), "that our friend Goldsmith had said to me, that he had come too late into the world, for that Pope and other poets had taken up the place in the Temple of Fame; so that, as but a few at any period can possess poetical reputation, a man of genius can now hardly acquire it. JOHNSON. 'That is one of the most sensible things I have ever heard of Goldsmith.' "

because he finally became tired of hearing Aristides called "the Just."

Themselves independent and original people, and hoping to conserve hard-won values, they especially felt the tensions, the contradictions, the embarrassments. "No man," said Johnson, "ever yet became great by imitation," and most of those rhinocerine sighs of his that recur throughout the critical writings have to do with the tedium, the abysmal lack of novelty or originality in one writer after another; and they alternate with quick appreciation of anything that showed an adventurous spirit.* He even projected, in a moment of burlesque, "a work to shew how small a quantity of REAL FICTION there is in the world," and how most writers persist in using "the same images, with very little variation." He took for granted – no one ever exposed it better – "the general conspiracy of human nature against contemporary merit." As for Edward Young's *Conjectures on Original Composition* (1759), which was to prove so inspiring a manifesto during the next seventy years, Johnson "was surprized," said Boswell, "to find Young receive as novelties what he thought very common maxims." No one was quicker than Johnson to damn the mere repetition of stock and received ideas. One thinks of his blunt dismissal of Lord Lyttelton's *Dialogues of the Dead*: "That man sat down to write a book, to tell the world what the world had all his life been telling him." Yet the same remark, uttered in a different tone of voice, could be applied to Johnson himself. For what most deeply

* E.g.: "*Familiar* images in laboured language"; "the merit of *original* thought is wanting . . ."; "He that courts his mistress in Roman imagery deserves to lose her"; "few images from *modern* life"; "of his images [Waller's mythological allusions] time has tarnished the splendour"; "the honour which is always due to an original writer"; "entitled to one praise of the highest kind . . . his mode of thinking and of expressing his thoughts is original." Johnson's position on this and related matters connected with our subject still remains generally unappreciated. The stock notion of it (still that inherited from the neo-romantics of Walter Pater's time) is if anything almost the reverse of the facts.

characterizes his writing might be described as common truths, deeply experienced and expressed with the passion and clarity of genius. So also with most of the other figures we mentioned. They could react with exasperated impatience to the repetition of familiar thoughts in familiar language. But they also knew that the pressure for novelty for its own sake could, in the long run, be more damaging to the arts. The great phrases in Johnson come immediately to mind: "the mind can only repose on the stability of truth"; "Shakespeare is above all writers, at least above all modern writers, the poet of nature, the poet who holds up to his readers a faithful mirror of manners and of life."

So with Voltaire, whose essay on taste, written for the *Encyclopédie* (1757) and soon translated and widely read in England, puts more strongly what we have already cited from Voltaire. If a period of art immediately behind us has little to be said for it, the pressure to be different can obviously be of value. But if "artists through the *apprehension* of being regarded as mere imitators" feel it necessary to "strike out into new and uncommon paths" after a really great period of art, the direction is almost certainly going to be downward. And Richard Hurd, in ending his long *Discourse on Poetical Imitation,* felt himself justified in one general conclusion which "they who have a comprehensive view of the history of letters, in their general periods, . . . will hardly dispute": that though many other causes may contribute to decline, "yet the *principal,* ever, is this *anxious dread of imitation* in polite and cultivated writers."

—11—

There are other reasons why Hume's analysis was not developed more than it was. To begin with, it made far more sense than other explanations. It was not so easy to dismiss or to cut down to size. The only relief was to forget it or at least not to dwell upon it. Yes, the real problem was not at all the grosser changes in "society" itself or in language (though these may be relevant). Neither was it Thomas Warton's suggestion that the Elizabethans were as creatively fertile as they were because there were not so many critics swarming about them. He may have had a point, and Goethe was also to imply as much.* But the truth was that never before had criticism — at least a substantial part of it — been so open and friendly as it was now to the idea of "genius" and "creativity." Neither was it quite convincing, except to those who wanted to be convinced, to say that the arts are being inevitably pushed into a corner because of the remorseless development of the analytic sciences. (A commonplace before the middle of the nineteenth century, this was to remain as a stock premise for the twentieth century.) It was a seductive explanation. But even the scientists, like Joseph Priestley, were not complaining that poetry was not "scientific" enough but rather that poetry seemed to them — from whatever obscure, self-defeating motive — to have begun to retreat from exactly those things (and of the broadest human concern) that the sciences, by definition, were not expecting to do. And that complaint was to continue as the authority and prestige of science grew throughout the next century and a half. As for audience generally: K. P. Moritz had a point when he mentioned the tailor's widow whose husband had married her because she read *Paradise Lost* with the right emphasis. It could be argued that the potential audience for poetry in the period from 1770 to 1830 was greater than it had ever been since the invention

* "Whoever will not believe," said Goethe, "that much of the greatness of Shakespeare is to be attributed to his great and powerful age need only ask himself whether he would think such a phenomenon possible in present-day England of 1824, in these wretched days of criticizing and fragmentizing journals . . . The critical sheets that daily appear in fifty different places, and the babble thereby occasioned in the public, allow nothing healthy to arise." (Eckermann, 2 January 1826.)

of printing — and not merely for Milton but for poetry now being written.*

Moreover, what Hume said was disturbing in another way. For if the other explanations were true, it could always be said that what they referred to was completely beyond human control, not only for human beings as individuals but collectively. If only a less advanced society can produce the greatest poetry — a poetry accessible to everyone — then this is a part of the price we must pay. And who, after all, would seriously want to live in Homeric Greece or in those societies where, as John Brown said, song, dance, legislation, and priesthood were united? — though perhaps some of those "second" or postprimitive periods were not so bad provided you could select the right station in life. In any case, we have no choice. And if language, as it becomes more denotative and abstract, inevitably loses its metaphoric power, there is again nothing we can do except to use our wits and try to make the best of the situation.

But nothing so distresses us as the thought that what we are deploring is not at all historically determined and necessary — the inevitable result or price of "civilized" or at least more "organized" society — but is, on the contrary, a *psychological* imposition of our own: the product of fears, of self-intimidations, and also (worst of all) of "values" — especially "originality" per se — that are in direct conflict with all those other values, classical and humanistic, that we are preaching or to which we are at least, in audience or congregation, giving Sunday-assent. In short we are thrown back upon ourselves and the realization that it is *we* who are collectively creating the circumstances we deplore, not as something necessary to cultural advancement but for other reasons. True, it could be said (as it could in every other protest against the social, moral,

* See below, p. 119.

military, or psychological structures created by man) that the individual is powerless. If other people insist on thinking and reacting this way, what are you as one individual able to do? But social and other forms of revolution do take place. Why do they seem easier to get started? Is it because there are really more people around for company and help? A William Blake could say: "Drive your cart and your plow over the bones of the dead." In this case, how many poets are really willing to live in such brave independence as Blake (not the same thing as living with the support of a coterie, however small), and, assuming they have the same commitment and single-mindedness of purpose that Blake had, also have the talent to keep themselves alive by doing other things, like painting or engraving? This is certainly one element in the chemistry of the situation. However much we talk about the inevitabilities or even the attractions of loneliness, which is so common a theme in the later eighteenth century, the fact remains – as Johnson so frequently points out – that few people are able to endure it in any fundamental way, at least for more than short stretches. And this compensatory effort of the middle- and later-eighteenth-century poet to make a virtue of solitude – forgivably prettifying, even falsifying it in self-protection – has a pathos that the historical and humane imagination should not reduce. Anyone who knew Greek – and a fair number of poets still did – knew also that our modern word "idiot" meant originally what is peculiar to a "private" person (probable cognates range from the Freudian "id" to our word "identity").

But was there not a far more fundamental problem? In social revolutions, one can really hate what one hopes to dislodge and replace. But could the poet or artist after 1750 really "hate," with true revolutionary fervor, Homer, Sophocles, Michelangelo, Shakespeare, or Milton, not to mention scores of others from the long, diverse past? Far from it. He admired them – if not all equally, at least a selective number. Is there not, built into the situation, a divided loyalty? How can we, in conscience, simply "plow over the bones of the dead"? Does not the essence of our heritage in the humanities and the arts involve the preservation of the best that has been so gradually, and against such odds, attained in the past? Would we, in the rapid changes now beginning to take place, really want a general amnesia, a brutal excision from our consciousness of all that has been so precariously won? Of course not. And in those great avuncular figures of the later eighteenth century who educate and usher in the next generation, and with it the beginning of the modern period generally – Johnson, Reynolds, Burke, and Gibbon in England, and, in Germany, Lessing, Goethe, Schiller – we feel constantly the effort to come to an understanding of the problem.

Meanwhile, in England especially, the poet since the death of Pope had staggered under the weight of the burden. "The languid strings," said Blake, "do scarcely move,/ The sound is forc'd, the notes are few." There is an unfinished drawing by Blake's friend, Henry Fuseli, that expresses the situation exactly – an almost surrealistically modern drawing (dated 1778–79) of the artist "moved by the grandeur" of the past. What is shown of the "grandeur" of the past is only the gigantic foot of some classical colossus and, above it, a great hand pointing upward. The modern artist cannot touch the hand. He is seated at the pedestal, half-bowed, with his left hand to his forehead, as if in despair. But his right arm is stretched out in caress, at once affectionate and helpless, over part of the colossal foot.

The English poetry of this period – a period more creative in poetry than we still (except for Blake and Burns) give it credit for being – cannot be sympathetically understood apart from what we have been saying. With some desperation, the poet was tempted to escort his volume into print – as we see some poets do now, if in other phrasing – with the apology that these were only private, minor jottings, and on special and admittedly restricted subjects. This had already been true since the 1730's, and was to become more so as the next century neared. So Coleridge, particularly sensitive as a barometer in his early years as a poet, could subtitle one of the "conversation poems": "A Poem Affecting Not To Be Poetry."

IV | The Third Temple

Yes, however seductive the arguments, it was plain that the principal difficulty for the modern poet or artist was not society and "unpoetic" customs and surroundings, not changes in language, not the growing compartmentalization of the mind and experience, competition from analytic philosophy and the sciences, nor the lack of "audience." In the eighteenth-century debate with itself, one after another of these considerations, not to mention others, had been brought forward, been given its due or more than its due, and been weighed in the balance. True, they were all important (this was taken for granted), and, if an art itself abandoned centrality, they would certainly become more so – particularly competition from other intellectual interests.

But the essential problem – the real anxiety – lay elsewhere, as David Hume had said, and it had to do with the artist's relation to his own art. It had to do with what the artist would least care to dwell on publicly if he were trying either to begin or even to maintain his way, and with what is even now – in the second half of the twentieth century – not openly declared but surrounded with a protective fog of other considerations: that is, his nakedness and embarrassment (with the inevitable temptations to paralysis or routine imitation, to retrenchment or mere fitful rebellion) before the amplitude of what two thousand years or more of an art had already been able to achieve. And meanwhile, with every generation, our sense of that amplitude – its variety in subject, in approach, in power or ingenuity of expression – has been further increasing as (justifiably, commendably) we continue to explore that heritage and extend our understanding of it. How could the poet or artist be expected to volunteer the confession that this was his first, his greatest problem? Who would afterwards give him a hearing – would think it worth the while to do so? The reaction, even in those who both valued the arts and sympathized with his plight, would be that of Joseph Priestley: in this case, stand aside; there is already more than enough from the past to occupy a longer life than any of us is given. No, one did not make one's entry into something so important — or try to maintain oneself in one's difficult middle years — by openly advertising one's inadequacies and dread of impotence, especially in a calling that one was by no means being forced to choose. Even Goethe, with far less of a national tradition in poetry to intimidate him, did not begin to speak freely until his old age, when he had behind him the confidence of acknowledged achievement and an established position in a national culture that no other poet or artist of the era attained in his own lifetime. Then he could talk more openly. In addition to that long statement of his about Shakespeare and the modern poet which we quoted in the first lecture,* we may cite two other remarks:

> It is certain that if everyone could be made aware early enough how full the world already is of things of highest excellence, and how much is required to set something beside those works that is equal to them, out of a hundred present-day poetic youths scarcely a single one would feel in himself enough perseverance, talent, and courage to go on peacefully and achieve a similar masterpiece. Many a young painter would never have taken a brush in hand if he had early enough known and conceived what a master like Raphael had already made (20 April 1825).

> Had I known [in writing *Werther* and *Faust*] as clearly as I now do how much that is excellent has been in existence for hundreds and thousands of years, I would not have written a line, but would have done something else (16 February 1826).

But, however reluctant he might be to acknowledge it, the artist himself knew — and knew far better than even so

* See above, pp. 5–6.

sympathetic a critic as Archibald Alison – that the real pressure on the artist to desert "the *end* of his art in his attempt to display his superiority in the art itself" was a pressure that came from within the art rather than from outside. (At least this was true in poetry and the visual arts, if not yet in music or in that promising, still enviably unselfconscious new form, the novel, so free now to appropriate whatever it would.) But for the poet to put his complaint in these terms was, as he instinctively knew, close to suicide. For he also knew, as Alison went on to say, how dependent he was, as he tried to get his bearings, on a sophisticated, increasingly specialized group of people – the vested interests seated in the first two rows, so to speak, and themselves as much the psychological product of the situation as he himself was except that they, by contrast, were happily spared the burden of execution. While they were ready to bludgeon him with comparisons with the amplitude and "originality" of the past, they were at the same time only too querulous about his ability or failure in establishing a new difference, or, as we now would say, a new "voice." Many of them were sympathetic; but when the cards were down, they appeared more sympathetic with the general plight of the poet than with what he felt able to do about it. It was no help at all, for example, to be told repeatedly what Emerson was to say a few years later: that Shakespeare and his contemporaries in the poetic drama were free to be and to do what they were and did because they were not yet shackled by our modern "petulant demand for originality" – that they could look upon "the mass of old plays" before them as only "waste stock, in which *any* experiment could be tried. Had the *prestige* which hedges about a modern tragedy existed, nothing could be done." You could warmly agree. But what were you to do? Treat Shakespeare himself and other writers in the same spirit as only so much "waste stock"? You might in a moment of madness or desperation try to do so, or pretend to do so. But you could be sure that the sympathy of those around you would begin to chill, and you could understand why.

There was, thought Alison, one way still possible of avoiding the otherwise inevitable bind (resulting in "the gradual desertion of the end of the art for the display of the art itself") – the "general diffusion of knowledge" through the spread of literacy. Whatever its liabilities, by "increasing in so great a proportion the number of judges," it could conceivably "*rescue* these arts from the sole dominion of the artists" and of those who surround them, demanding specialism, difference, or refinement because of the same psychological pressures. What Alison was saying is what Johnson had so often implied a few years before, when he spoke of the value of the "common reader" – the reader still "*uncorrupted* with literary prejudices." *

Could this still be possible? Could the artist still reach home to an audience that could in some way help him to skip over the self-created rim that, through no fault or lack of his own, seemed to be encircling him? There seemed little hope otherwise for "rescue" of the arts back into centrality of social or generally human importance, and less hope if one looked ahead to the future. For something relatively new in the history of the arts had begun to take place during the eighteenth century (new to anything like a comparable degree); and if you allowed yourself to dwell on it, you could only assume it was destined to increase.

* So a century later Thomas Mann's "Dr. Faustus" (the composer Adrian Leverkühn), convinced that serious music has now become "too difficult to write," speculates: "Isn't it amusing that this art for a long time considered itself a means of release, whereas it itself, like all the arts, needs to be redeemed from a pompous isolation which was the fault of the culture-emancipation, the elevation of culture as substitute for religion – from being alone with an elite of culture . . . which will soon no longer be . . . so that art will soon be entirely alone, alone to die, unless it is to find its way to the folk." (*Dr. Faustus,* chapter xxxi.)

This was what threatened to become a radical split between "sophisticated" and "popular" taste in the arts. In the process each would become drastically impoverished, and the isolation of each could be expected to increase further through the growing postures and inevitable rigidities of self-defense. And one of the results, already beginning, would be the development among the "sophisticated" of what we now tend to call a "subculture" – and a subculture of a peculiar and also of a potentially (perhaps in time a helplessly) self-defeating kind.

What was both fundamental and new about this split between "sophisticated" and "popular" taste was that, for the first time on an important scale, the essential difference had to do not merely – not even primarily – with the actual qualities, or degree of quality, of a work of art but rather with something else: that is, sheer chronological *priority*. As a result, you could ironically have a situation where "sophisticated" taste would find itself forced to turn (whatever its theoretical professions) not only against the "popular" but even against what the informed humanist and critic himself espouses in the great art of the past. All this had been implied in what David Hume had said, in the middle of the eighteenth century, and it was now picked up and rephrased in the early 1800's by an enlightened pupil of Hume, Francis Jeffrey, certainly one of the shrewdest critical minds of the time and in our own century one of the most underrated.* In the gap now

* Underrated partly because of the quotable crispness with which he opened his famous review of Wordsworth's *Excursion* ("This will never do"). That phrase is remembered even by those who have never themselves gone through the *Excursion*, or, if they have, hardly think of it as a model for the greater poetry of the future.

Jeffrey is particularly relevant to our present subject – the drama of our approach to the inherited past. He is one of the last of that remarkable group of Scotsmen (Hume himself, Blackwell, Duff, Gerard, Blair, Kames, Adam Smith, Monboddo, Alison, John Wilson) who, from the middle eighteenth century through the early nineteenth, serve as a kind of Greek chorus commenting on the course of English literature and the widening between "popular" taste and the "refined and fastidious" critic (Jeffrey is writing this in 1810 – he is discussing what Sir Walter Scott, in narrative poems like the "Lady of the Lake," was trying to do), the real problem is not in what we all say we "substantially" want in poetry. In fact at this time (the early 1800's, when so many were still eager to read poetry), you could truthfully say that the "most popular passages in popular poetry" are usually the most "beautiful and striking" – and would be admitted to be such by the critic if only he had not read anything like them before. People now are not *potentially* so different from what they were in those cherished ages in the past when we say that popular taste (by contrast with the present) could directly share in and respond to a great art. To the unsophisticated, said Jeffrey, even the twentieth imitation or repetition will have "all the charm of an original" (and was this not also true of the "popular" in those "golden" eras to which we look back with such persistent nostalgia?). But the fastidious reader now finds all this "trite or hackneyed," whether he really wants to end up in this situation or not. In other words, it is not "because the ornaments of popular poetry are deficient in *intrinsic* worth and beauty that they are slighted by the

---

arts generally in their own time: half-removed but not, at their best, too parochially defensive; less crushed than the English themselves by the weight of the great English past, but still in love with its tradition and eager to share in the mystery of its fertility. (Defensiveness, of course, does exist, and with it the temptation at times to beat, or threaten to beat, the English present with the club of the English past and to imply that some of the pristine virtues, if less vigorous now in the homeland, are actively present elsewhere and are ready to make their contribution.) Much of the fascination of the group is that they serve as the prototype of what still remains unexplored in any really comprehensive sense (the subject is unique to English as contrasted with every other European literature): the relation, during the last century and a half, of the vastly expanded English-speaking world (in population now twenty times that of the Britain of 1800) to the vertically long, if geographically confined, creativity of English letters from the beginning to at least the mid-nineteenth century.

critical reader" but simply because the eye and ear of the "critical" are "palled by repetition," and what we think of as "sophisticated" taste automatically begins to compare what is being done with what has already been done. And what is said here about "language" and "expression," or all that we now try to suggest by the word "idiom," applies also to the treatment of character, to the drama of incident and human interplay, and to the unembarrassed freedom of poetry to turn directly to larger issues without inhibition or the self-defensive specialisms and insect-dance of indirectness.

But could it not be argued (I am not now paraphrasing Jeffrey) that this particular kind of split between "sophisticated" and "popular" prevented – by its very nature – any genuine hope of "rescue" through the active cooperation of the "popular"? The very fact that neither (at least as of 1750–1830) disagreed "substantially" or theoretically about what was wanted in poetry paradoxically made the chasm between them all the less bridgeable. For it already proved that "intrinsic" qualities in art – though ostensibly valued in common – could not, by themselves, provide genuine ground for agreement; that the real point at issue was something else superadded by the sophisticated – something that, by definition, could work against the "intrinsic" simply by progressively removing it from the currency as usable coin. In this case, how confidently could the poet turn to the "popular" voice? What for the "popular" was wanted, what he himself had most loved when he had first turned to poetry, was constantly in the process of becoming "alms for oblivion" – not, of course, to the memory or the idealizing imagination, but for his own practical use. Moreover, was not the poet himself – however he might loathe the idea of being left isolated within a "subculture" – half committed to the same kind of premise, self-destructive as it might prove to be? He naturally wished to make a contribution of his own. Even Keats — the freest of all the major Romantics from envy of the past and the most idealistic about the "immortal free-masonry" of the great in any age — said, when his friends justly praised the first *Hyperion* as equal to Milton as far as it went, that he did not want to write a poem as if by Milton but only as if by Keats.

Jeffrey's own prediction is that the premium the sophisticated place on mere priority is bound to spread with the growth of literacy and education, and that in time we shall have almost everyone with any interest in the arts, real or pretended, sharing much the same reaction, or at least parroting the same demand. In short, if the modern chasm between what we here call "sophisticated" and "popular" is someday likely to narrow, Jeffrey's prognosis is not reassuring. It will narrow not because of the creative use or resurgence of the "popular" as active copartner (though Jeffrey welcomes what Walter Scott is trying to do now). It will happen only because of the fading and final retreat of the "popular" as an important force. The field will simply be left to the "sophisticated" and to its extending fringe of suburbs, while what is left of the "popular," in the older sense, will move progressively outside the pale — lacking voice or confidence and inevitably turning to other things. The interested reader still "uncorrupted" — to use Johnson's phrase — "by literary prejudices" will simply not be there, at least as a factor worth considering.

In the situation now taking shape, said Jeffrey, "Whatever may be gained or lost, it is obvious that poetry must become less popular by means of it: For the most natural and obvious manner is always the most taking; and whatever costs the author much pains and labour is usually found to require a corresponding effort on the part of the reader." And Jeffrey takes up the alternatives that appear to be left to the "modern poet . . . debarred by the lavishness of his predecessors" and proscribed as he is by the "dread of imitation" from an open use of common "subjects, situations, and images," or even a healthy and free directness of "manner and tone." The alternatives ahead for the poet seem to be the following: an increasing and more detailed realism in the study and presentation of character; a more careful (but more "limited") exploration of the emotional life; and, third, a self-conscious "distortion" of object and idiom, either by "affectation" of an obvious sort or through "dissecting" a subject – or a "narrow corner" of it – "with such curious and microscopic accuracy" that its "original form" is "no longer discernible to the eyes of the uninstructed." Elsewhere Jeffrey speculates that the promising new genre of the novel will give us something of what we find in the great dramatic poetry of the Elizabethans and Jacobeans. But how can we avoid assuming that what is now being said about "poetry" – about verse as contrasted with prose – will not in time apply equally to the novel itself?

—3—

In short, one kept coming back to what Hume had said about emulation in the arts – what promotes, twists, or dampens it. This was the point from which one always seemed to start: perhaps not in one's speculative thinking about art (who really wished to dwell on it, or least of all on its future implications? – for what could one do about it?), but it was the point from which one started in actual feeling if he was even half honest to the pinch of the situation – or even if he was not. For after the merely theoretical issues had been aired for whatever purpose and with whatever gain or loss, this was the situation that confronted the writer as soon as he returned to his closet to face that intimidating object, the blank sheet of paper waiting to be filled.

And in one important way the embarrassment for the poet had sharpened during the fifty years since Hume had written. The whole concept of "originality" had both deepened and spread – deepened as a hold on the conscience and spread horizontally among the literate, and the peripheries of the literate, as something desired per se. Back in the 1730's and 1740's, when the neoclassic had begun to reconsider its own self-limitations, the idea of "originality" had understandably been plucked out into prominence as one way of describing what was felt to be most missing. It had every advantage for that purpose. It was an "open" term, capable of suggesting not only creativity, invention, or mere priority but also essentialism (getting back to the fundamental), vigor, purity, and above all freedom of the spirit. As such it transcended most of the particular qualities that could be latched on to it, qualities that, if taken singly as exclusive ends, could so easily conflict with each other (priority versus essentialism, for instance, or the inevitable confinements of "purity" versus "range," or primitive simplicity versus the creative intelligence of an Isaac Newton). Add to this the social appeal of the concept of "originality": its association with the individual's "identity" (a word that was now increasing in connotative importance) as contrasted with the more repressive and dehumanizing aspects of organized life. What Lionel Trilling rightly describes as one of the principal themes of modern literature – the growing disenchantment of culture with culture itself – had already begun in the second third of the eighteenth century. If for a while the undercult of "originality" seemed like an emotional jag (and it was), even that side of it has more than the interest it used to have for us as merely part of the picturesque folklore of the eighteenth century. We now see it as an anticipation of what the present emerging generation is experiencing, two centuries later, in its own reaction to a half-century of brilliant formalization in sophisticated art and, more important, to what it conceives to be the dehumanizing pressures of an organized and increasingly crowded society.

In any case the spread of the idea of "originality" into the fringes of behavior and into stock value or stock response was only a symptom of the grip that the ideal was beginning to take on the center of the intellect itself. For the concept of "originality" meshed with so many other things in life aside from the arts (especially the concept of progress in the cumulative sciences, social and historical as well as physical) that the conscience was trapped by it now as it had earlier been trapped by the neoclassic use of the classical example. In short, the conscience had taken another Trojan Horse into the walls, from which the unexpected again appeared. By the 1750's some of the least original minds of the time were beginning to prate constantly of "originality," thus setting a precedent with which the intellectual has since been condemned to live. True, almost every major mind could protest against the new bind that the fetish of originality would create for the arts; could say repeatedly (as had their neoclassic forebears) that this — which they themselves had advocated — could become as much a tyranny to the human spirit as what they themselves had earlier reacted against. But ideas evolved for a special purpose and under special circumstances have a way, as Burke said, of being snatched out of one's hands by others who have shared little of the experience or imagination of those who first advanced them. The slightest reflection should remind us that "originality" in the arts need not imply vigor, range, or even openness of mind — or power of language or anything else of a qualitative nature. Repeatedly this is said, and with a sadder, more experienced spirit than by the neoclassic critics a century before. But it could always be answered that men like Johnson, Burke, Voltaire, or Goethe could afford to talk this way. Their battle for insight before the rising multiplicity of experience and achievement was already won, or half won. And, in any case, did not they themselves take for granted the basic psychological fact that, unless the scene is shifted – unless the kaleidoscope is turned, with the pieces tumbling into another pattern – the mind falls asleep, and ceases even to notice? Novelty, said Aristotle long ago, has at least this merit: it reawakens attention. Of course they knew this. (One had only to open Johnson to find this realization implied on every page of his greater writing – though counterbalanced by other considerations.)

In short, the eighteenth century, in its effort to lift the burden of the past or to shift it to one side, had first spun off, then developed as a specific value, and finally elevated to the status of ideal that merely open and elusive (indeed potentially self-contradictory) premise of "originality." True, the period was also beginning to develop antibodies, so to speak, to what a part of itself was preaching. We must return to this later. And it did, after all, train up and give a start to what we think of as the whole romantic and generally nineteenth-century movement in the arts, for which, extending Dryden's imaginative metaphor of "The Second Temple" for the neoclassic, we have suggested "The Third Temple" as shorthand. But in any case the fact remained that the eighteenth-century "Enlightenment" had created, and had foisted upon itself and its immediate child – not to mention its later descendants – an ideal of "originality" sanctioned both officially (theoretically, intellectually) and, *in potentia*, popularly. As a result the vulnerability of the poet, already great enough, was accentuated by having his uneasiness now given a "local habitation and a name." For the first time in history, the ideal of "originality" – aside from the personal pressures the artist might feel to achieve it anyway — was now becoming defined as necessary, indeed taken for granted. At the same time, as an additional embarrassment, the eighteenth-century effort to clear its own mind and to reground itself in the fundamental — to go back to the essentially human, as we ourselves are again trying to do — had evolved for the artist an ancillary ideal: that of *sincerity*.

—4—

These two relatively new ideals of "originality" and "sincerity" (new at least for art) were henceforth to lie heavily on the shoulders of almost every English-speaking writer, and very soon almost every Western artist. And like most compensatory ideals that become rigid through anxiety, they only complicated the problem further (and, for that matter, also conflicted with each other). They both quickly became the sort of ideals that you can neither live with nor live without. You cannot openly deny them. You cannot afford to come out and say that you want to be "unoriginal" or "insincere." Yet if you are never to write a line unless you are convinced that you are totally "sincere," then when do you start? You can be sure that something is going to happen both to your fluency and your range. David Perkins, in his *Wordsworth and the Poetry of Sincerity*, has shown the dilemma that Wordsworth inherited and then — through his own individual success — powerfully deepened. Similarly, if you are exhorted to be "original" at all costs, how do you take even the first step — especially if what you have been taught most to admire (and what in fact you really do most admire) is best typified by those very predecessors from whom you must now distinguish yourself, and, even worse, if your "original" departure from those admired models must spring from an "originality" that is itself "sincere"?

This was the fearful legacy to the great Romantics who

come at the close of the eighteenth century — who in this, as in so many other ways, are so much the children of the eighteenth century: a legacy that consisted of not just one but a whole series of conflicting demands. Meanwhile, as the eighteenth century passed into the nineteenth, the finest critical intelligence of the time — English, Scottish, German — continued to turn, with even more delicacy and historical understanding than before, to the highest moments of the English Renaissance. Hazlitt, with sharp impatience, weighed the modern movement against the condensed ideal of that past. The title of his essay "Why the Arts Are Not Progressive" suggests a point of view that persists through every critical work he wrote and is all the more persuasive because of his robust liberalism. And his pupil John Keats — easily the greatest example in any country of what Romanticism might hope from the self-taught, or the half-self-taught — spoke of Hazlitt's "depth of taste" as one of the three most formative things to touch him (he says this at the age of twenty-two, at the very point where his own astonishing career begins), and wrote of the "egotism" with which the modern movement, in its forgivable (perhaps desirable) retrenchment to the personal, still threatened to "circumscribe" or strangle art: "We must cut this . . . Let us have the old Poets." He himself was determined to be a free agent: "Why should we be owls" — wise and contemplative perhaps but blind in the daylight — "when we *can* be eagles." But with the good sense that was one side of his imaginative endowment, he by no means minimized the problems ahead. The drama of his development from here to the end involves an open — and progressively successful — struggle with them. Wordsworth, with that valuable self-confidence which could still plow its own way and which led Hazlitt, however he deplored the way, to doff his hat to him and consider him, for this very reason, the greatest English poet of the time, could say in a testy moment that "anybody could write like Shakespeare if he had a mind to." (Yes, said Charles Lamb, all one needs is the "mind.") But even Wordsworth had more difficulties in getting started or renewing his efforts than he cared to advertise. Coleridge, for his part, had, by his late twenties, ended with an ideal of poetry according to which, as he "freely" admitted, he was himself no poet at all – an ideal that looked back to the great poetic dramas of another era. As his brother George said, Coleridge had even as a youth found it "embarrassing" to try to write seriously when he appreciated so vividly, and could explicate so brilliantly, the great poetry of the past. For a really major poem – an "epic" or something like it – Coleridge writes that he would need at least twenty years. Commendably he lists the subjects needed as background: mathematics, and then "Optics and Astronomy, Botany, Metallurgy, Fossilism, Chemistry, Geology, Anatomy, Medicine – then the *mind of man* – then the *minds of men* – in all Travels, Voyages, and Histories." And this would be only the start; for all this must be subsumed, distilled, and then the further challenge would begin – how to wring or create from this a poetry at once capacious, humanly and morally relevant, richly nuanced and impassioned, yet intellectually and imaginatively unified and sustained; and then (hardest of all) to do this with a *difference,* without echo and vulnerability to the charge of imitation. Meanwhile he himself was only a bird of one of the more awkward, less attractive species (he loved to play with these comparisons): vulnerable, perhaps well-meaning like the albatross, but usually with a small or croaking voice. Or, most frequently of all, an ostrich: "I have too clearly before me the idea of a poet's genius to deem myself other than a very humble poet; but in the very *possession* of the idea . . . I can understand and interpret a poem in the spirit of poetry." Then he goes on: "Like the ostrich, I cannot fly, yet have I wings that give me the *feeling* of flight," and he pictures himself running along the plain, looking up to the birds that really can fly — from eagles to mere larks — and sharing empathically what the "experience" of being a poet can mean. By the time he was forty-one he confessed that because of the special problem of the need to establish difference he had "for many years past given [poetry] up in despair." * It was once again the major figures who felt this anxiety to the full. (Robert Southey, like Sir Richard Blackmore a century before, could continue to grind out long epics, as much from conscientious idealism as from imperviousness to self-doubt.)

—5—

Was there no way of getting out of this self-created prison? For of course it *was* self-created. How the Oriental artist, during all the centuries that he followed his craft, would have stared — or laughed — if told that those past artists by whom, and through whom, he had been taught should suddenly represent territory that was *verboten*: that he had studied them only in order to be different! Take any of the great past eras we say we most admire: would not the Greek artist, the Renaissance artist, be complimented if told he could be virtually mistaken for his greatest predecessors; and, if he was able to go still further than they, did he not assume that it would be through assimilating the virtues and techniques of his predecessors while perhaps capping them with just a little more? Was it not a sufficient triumph even to recapture a few of the

* Even throughout the last century alone, he says, "so countless have been the poetic metamorphoses of almost all possible thoughts and connections of thought, that it is scarcely practicable for a man to write in the ornamental style on any subject" without echoing unconsciously or appearing to imitate; "and this it is which makes poetry so very difficult, because so very easy, in the present day. I myself have for many years past given it up in despair." (Letter to Thomas Curnik, 9 April 1814.)

virtues of our greatest predecessors, as Sir Joshua Reynolds said in his last discourse to the students at the Royal Academy? — that last discourse in which he disowned his earlier willingness to abide by "the taste of the times in which I live" and said that, "however unequal I feel myself to that attempt, were I now to begin the world again, I would tread in the steps of that great master [Michelangelo] . . . To catch the slightest of his perfections would be glory and distinction enough." It requires no heroic effort to be different from the great.

Nature — life in all its diversity — is still constantly before us. Cannot we *force* ourselves to turn directly toward it? And some of the Romantics tried to do just that. I quote, because it is so short, a remark from a letter of the painter John Constable (31 October 1820): "In the early ages of the fine arts, the productions were more affecting and sublime." And why? Only because "the artists, being without human exemplars, *were forced to have recourse to nature*." "Force yourselves to have that recourse" was, in effect, the advice of two of the greatest men of letters that the eighteenth century produced — Johnson and Goethe. Over and over again, though Johnson allowed Imlac in *Rasselas* to admit that "the first writers took possession of the most striking objects," he himself kept stressing that "there are qualities in . . . nature *yet* undiscovered, and combinations in the powers of art yet untried." Granted (in fact it is tautological) that over-all characteristics remain the same. But the poet — to refer again to a passage quoted before — can still observe the "alterations" that "time is always making in the modes of life." The complaint "that all topics are pre-occupied" is repeated only by the timid or by the militantly conservative, a complaint "by which some discourage others and some themselves." And Goethe could point out the radical mistake of the new "subjective" writer who concentrates solely on expressing his individual feelings in his frantic hope of being "original." He will have "soon talked out his little *internal* material, and will at last be ruined by mannerism," by the mere repetition of what his small inner fountain provides, while the poet who turns bravely and directly to nature, to external reality, will tap a perennial fountain of subject matter and, in doing so, become "inexhaustible and forever new."

And to an important extent that salutary counsel was followed. But problems still remained – problems that sharply anticipate those that we now face a century later. Take just one. Assume that you can still pull yourself up by your bootstraps and can energetically and freshly begin, by some miracle, to write in the "larger genres" of poetry – the epic, poetic drama, or at least analogous equivalents. There is still the fact that your audiences, your readers, are different now from what they were in the past. At least they threaten to be so. Even if they, and the critics who assail you, could somehow put "originality" out of their minds (which you can be sure they will not), and could be as open as they enthusiastically say that Shakespeare's audience was, is it not also a fact that this more literate modern audience, living in its more complex world, has been deriving its own "imaginative exercise" – its *katharsis,* to use Aristotle's term – from literature itself, from the large accumulated heritage of imaginative literature? Hazlitt shrewdly raised that question in his essay "On Modern Comedy." The Aristotelian *katharsis* that comes in seeing a great tragedy (with us it too often comes in merely *reading* great tragedies) "substitutes an *artificial and intellectual* interest for real passion." It does this automatically. But in that case we could say that

Tragedy, like Comedy, must therefore defeat itself; for its patterns must be drawn from the living models within the breast, from feeling or from observation; and the materials

> of Tragedy cannot be found among a people, who are the habitual spectators of Tragedy, whose interests and passions are not their own, but ideal, remote, sentimental, and abstracted. It is for this reason chiefly, we conceive, that the highest efforts of the Tragic Muse are in general the earliest; where the strong impulses of nature are not lost in the refinements and glosses of art.

And John Wilson could develop, from this premise, a question that would strike home to every poet of the time (and still more to every poet since). The human imagination, when both fed and challenged constantly by a rich but unsystematized life, may move freely and instinctively into the "larger genres," in its hope to convey or understand its experience. But if the habitual daily use of our imaginations (no longer submitting to *real* life and no longer constantly dwelling in the mesh of it) turns largely for compensatory nourishment and exercise to past poetry, shall we not end with merely a lyric — or, if not lyric, at least a shorter-breathed — poetry, a poetry produced largely from the soil of past poetry? Of course. With this more concentrated idealization — a concentration distilled from generations of previous fictional and imaginative concentrations — had already arisen the almost tyrannic concept of "pure poetry" that we discussed earlier.* And whatever the romantic success with the lyric — and its success with the "greater" lyric is probably, given the same span of time, unequaled — there was one major cost difficult to deny, a cost recognized by the major poets themselves who at the time and since have repeatedly — with indisputable gain to themselves as well as to poetry itself — struggled to break out of the lyric into a wider field. The cost is that "shorter" forms, however suitable for the expression of mood or the development of a few themes, are not — or still do not seem to the poet to be — suited as the vehicle

* See above, pp. 74–75.

of a comprehensive point of view. Much less can the shorter forms present "nature" or the outer world in a diverse or ranging way, at least with the unity that is simultaneously prized. For this some more capacious genre is required, and the history of poetry from the romantic period to the present shows a persistent quest for it. If the "greater genres" are inaccessible, and narrative poetry is more or less (and increasingly) ruled out by the competition of the novel, what then is left? What, more particularly, is left when the poet himself, even in a long poem, is unwilling to surrender lyric condensation and intensity? Attempts have been innumerable, and would include such diverse results as *The Prelude, Childe Harold, Prometheus Unbound, In Memoriam, Modern Love, The Bridge, Patterson, Four Quartets,* and the *Cantos*. The list includes some of the most impressive poems of the modern world, and yet in one sense the search for a form has not been successful. For all these poems are *ad hoc* experiments that have not been repeated. No new genre has really established itself. Though the subject matter could be to some degree externalized through a symbol, as in Keats's odes or Wordsworth's descriptions of landscape, it remains generally true that this poetry is getting comparatively less help from its subject and, for just that reason, is placing a heavier demand on the poet's language. A poetry that cannot, in Hazlitt's phrase, "share the palm with its subject" must, if it is to succeed, sustain an especially high level of powerful phrasing. Thus the romantic poets themselves confronted for the first time and left to their followers the problem of attaining the scope and diversity of a major expression within an essentially lyrical habit of mind and for an audience that – by the later nineteenth century – had come to expect, and still expects, lyricism. Or, if "lyricism" is self-defensively rejected – as often in the twentieth century's effort to get the Romantics off its back — the rejection involves no real transcendence of the limitation of the "shorter" forms but only the uneasy discard, in the spirit of what Santayana called "penitent art" (art disowning its powers to please and putting on sackcloth and ashes), of some of the romantic virtues of lyricism, in particular the romantic ideal of the union of lyrical music or cadence with impassioned and suggestive power of phrase.

The drama of the historical development of twentieth-century poetry must be viewed in the light of its own uneasiness about its inheritance of the romantic lyric — with many of the premises still shared and certainly with the same premium on condensation, but with the conviction that this particular resolution cannot again be repeated for the simple reason that we now have this too behind us as a further addition to our own, still heavier "burden of the past," a burden that can truthfully be said to exist only in the imagination but is nonetheless present. We are of imagination all compact.

—6—

And yet, with all the strikes against them, the greater Romantics still succeeded (astonishingly, when we remember that in England we are dealing with only some twenty-five or thirty years, in a nation with about a twenty-fifth of the population of the English-speaking world now). To try to touch on what each of them did would demand not only another lecture but a series of lectures, and ideally a step-by-step biography of the drama of each writer's life. I use this moment to plead for a more sympathetic — a more psychologically and a more literarily informed — use of biography: a recognition of what the artist confronted in what were for him the most important things with which to struggle (his craft and his whole relation with tradition, with what has been done and with what he hopes can still be done). In comparison, so much to which we confine ourselves in literary biography is far less relevant – no more relevant than it would be for any number of other people who had devoted their years to doing radically different things, or for that matter to doing nothing. (It is like assuming, as Coleridge said, that every "deer-stealer" had it in him to become a Shakespeare.) Strangely, biographies of statesmen or scientists (or artists in other fields) are less guilty of this reductionism to the "deer-stealer" approach, and will focus primarily on what the man really did, why and how he was great: the situation he inherited and his struggle with that inheritance. Why are we alone so shy of the essential? As with biography, so with the reconsideration of literary history itself that we now seem about to make: here too these concerns could profitably be nearer the center of our thinking.

If we are forced to try to answer our question in a few sentences, we have only to repeat the clichés about Romanticism – but with a special imaginative sympathy for the particular question we have been discussing here – and we can get a tolerable notion of what at least permitted, if it did not create, this remarkable end-product of the eighteenth century, which provided the creative capital off which the nineteenth century and much of the twentieth (though in the latter case uneasily) has continued to live. For example, one answer is surely to be found in the opening up of new subject matters where the challenge of the past was less oppressive: simple life (of which there were to be twentieth-century urban as well as romantically rural varieties), children, the poor and socially slighted; landscape and scenery; such inward experiences as revery, dream, and mysticism; the whole concept of the "strange" either to awaken attention through difference in mode or phrase, to explore something really new, or to provide setting and focus for familiar nostalgia; the past itself in periods or ways not previously exploited by the traditional genres; the geographically remote or unusual, or conversely its apparent opposite (for example, Wordsworth; or the young Emerson on the central challenge of the age: "I ask not for the great, the remote . . . I embrace the common, I explore and sit at the feet of the familiar, the low"). Every attempt to "define" Romanticism in the light of subject is doomed to failure except as it applies to a limited part. For the opening of new subject matters, as of approach, proceeds in almost every direction, like spokes pointing outward from the hub of a wheel but with no rim to encase them. The one thing they all have in common is an interest or hope in the hitherto unexploited. And despite the strong attraction of twentieth-century post-romantic formalism to ideals of retrenchment and self-limitation, that still remains with us as a premise with which we are disinclined to quarrel.

Then there is the new particularity even in the treatment of traditional or familiar subjects; philosophically, psychologically, emotionally, stylistically, Romanticism can be partly, by no means wholly, described as a protest on behalf of particularity and concreteness. The potential release this offered to art and to the mind generally was constantly being pointed out from the 1750's on. Turn directly enough to nature in all its shadings (to paraphrase Goethe again), and the anxiety to be "original" will be cured: the new will come of itself. The only problem to the artist is to be sufficiently open. And it took some time for this to happen. It did not come easily. We do not explain the results, as I for years tried to do, by leaping with both feet into the history of formal British empirical philosophy from Locke through Hume. So much else also enters into the picture: above all the long, conscientious neoclassic revaluation of itself, its reweighing of itself in the balance against the "classical," and its growing repudiation of part of what it had done (for example, Johnson's rejection, on broadly classical grounds, of the dogma of the dramatic unities and other neoclassic rules of decorum); its realization – as we see in men like Johnson, Reynolds, or Goethe – of the tyranny of its own essentialism with its compulsive (and in its own way deeply nostalgic) clutch toward generality and purged or distilled abstraction. True, you could also have in time a reverse tyranny – as men again like Johnson, Reynolds, Goethe, Hazlitt, and Keats foresaw – a tyranny now of the trivial. But this was not yet a significant danger. It was a special strength of the romantic poets that they were able to carry through these developments without surrendering the older ideals of poetry as the representing of "general nature" and while still ministering to the human hunger for concrete relevance and personal meaning. Widening and deepening the notion of "nature," they continued at their best to focus on the point where the personal dawns into the general and fact is exhibited, in Whitehead's phrase, with "a highlight thrown on what is relevant to its preciousness." And of course we all still subscribe to this as a premise, even though the twentieth century has been or until recently was inclined to question the Romantics sharply (not wholly on philosophic grounds) in those special forms of achievement where they most succeeded.

—7—

The new subject matters and the new uses of particularity appear in romantic art and literature in every country. Moreover, they form a common bond between writers otherwise so different as the apocalyptic Blake and the antiquarian Scott, or the transcendentalists and the worldly, skeptical Byron. To these two characteristics we should add a third – less generally acknowledged and appreciated by us now than are the others, and for reasons not entirely to our credit. Yet to the dispassionate observer, concerned not only with "Romanticism" but with the arts generally from the 1750's to the first World War, it would leap to the eye – one would think – as one of the three or four most distinctive things that could be said about the arts throughout this period.

I refer to the remarkably "open" – even obvious – idiom of the arts, including music and the novel, during this century and a half, and to the frankly popular stance of the nineteenth-century movement as a whole. Think of the large concert halls and opera houses, and the kinds of music that permitted them; the leap into mass circulation of the novel, including many we ourselves continue to prize and hold up as models of what must now be avoided because of their very success in doing what they did (remember those crowds that stood at the wharfs in places like Boston and New York to get the latest installment of a Dickens novel); and above all the large public for poetry that begins to dwindle only near the end of the century. If a poem did catch on, it brought returns that now seem to us incredible. The publisher of Cowper's *The Task* made a profit of £10,000 (almost $300,000 in present purchasing power). Longman gave Tom Moore, for *Lalla Rookh*, what would now amount to $50,000, and Murray offered the same sum to George Crabbe for *Tales of the Hall* and half as much to Byron for a single canto of *Childe Harold*. A generation later, Longfellow's *Courtship of Myles Standish* was to sell ten thousand copies in one day in London alone, though the subject was not particularly familiar to English readers and though the novel had long since become the dominant form for narrative and was indeed fast becoming the dominant literary form generally. These were exceptions, of course. Any one volume was a gamble. But there were plenty of publishers ready to take it. Keats's hope not only to support himself by his poetry but also to travel widely, without benefit of fellowship or grant, was by no means unreasonable. Our point is not that "greatness" in art and "popularity" have suddenly become synonymous, as they seemed to the nostalgic imagination to have been in the primitive "Iron" and postprimitive "Golden" ages. Far from it. The point is only the openness of idiom that prevents the assumption, whether affected or genuinely despondent, that the two are mutually exclusive – and prevents it despite the deterministic arguments we summarized about the modern split between "sophisticated" and "popular" art. Ortega y Gasset rightly ridiculed those in the 1910's and 1920's who, psychologically oblivious of all that underlay the desperate antipopular stance of the post-romantic reaction, met the issue by simply denying it: by routinely misapplying the elementary reflection that all change is by definition "unpopular" and then pointing to the stormy reception of Victor Hugo's *Hernani,* to the audiences that expressed shock at Beethoven or Wagner, or to those who did not like the *Lyrical Ballads.* You know the argument. For it still goes on. It takes the form of a crude syllogism, each step of which is full of holes: The new is automatically opposed simply because it is new, at least unfamiliar, and is consequently "unpopular." Now neither *Finnegans Wake* nor the *Lyrical Ballads* (the examples can be multiplied *ad infinitum*) was immediately embraced with warmth by the many. *Ergo,* the problem they face in reception is the same, and all that either needs is for the shock of strangeness to wear off, thus permitting them to become a part of our habitual responses. One thinks of that line Coleridge was so fond of quoting: "And coxcombs vanquish Berkeley with a grin." Of course Ortega is right. When there were protests against the rising wave of Romanticism a century and a half ago, it was not because it was elitist, artificially "difficult," and restricted to the understanding or joys of the initiated few, but for reasons directly opposite.

We cited earlier the belief that there was one possibility for "rescue" of the arts back into centrality — an appeal over the heads of the "sophisticated" to the "popular" — and we also mentioned the theoretical doubts expressed about the likelihood of its happening. But as Imlac in *Rasselas* says about the problem of getting out of the prison of the "happy valley," "Many things difficult to design prove easy to performance." And Hazlitt liked to cite the philosopher who, weary of arguing against Zeno's paradox proving the impossibility of motion, finally rose and walked across the room. To an important extent that "rescue" of the arts through the extension of their public did happen, against all the theoretical probabilities, and was to continue to happen throughout the nineteenth century. Nor was it simply bestowed by social circumstance. It had to be won.* Whatever else can be said of Romanticism, it ushered in — indeed involved — the most sustained effort of the last three centuries to secure a popular appeal for the serious arts. If there is no significant aspect of Romanticism on which we have dwelt less, it is partly because of the inferred rebuke to ourselves. For the romantic effort, with its remarkable if emotionally specialized success, was to create an immense problem for the twentieth century in its own traumatic attempt to disengage itself from the nineteenth. Forced to establish and defend a difference, the twentieth century was led into a situation where — as Ortega y Gasset predicted in *The Dehumanization of the Arts* — it often found itself compelled to champion the anti-popular (humanly confusing

* Comments about the growth of literacy, the rising middle class, and so on have a point. But the twentieth century has seen a further extension of these circumstances at a time when much of what we call "serious" art has been frankly, if unwillingly, directed to subcultures and to the academy.

the "*anti*-popular" with the merely "a-popular" or the "unpopular"), without either wanting to do so or quite knowing why it was doing so. Adding to the psychological conflict was the fact that the twentieth-century artist, with few exceptions, continued to share the humanitarian and social liberalism of the romantic. If forced to defend the concept of an elitist art – self-consciously refined or specialized in idiom – he was therefore a divided soul. In any case he lacked the aristocratic milieu and the intellectual confidence that had sustained the neoclassic artist in the late 1600's when he had turned to the building of what Dryden called "The Second Temple." The modern could not even turn with much heart, as could the neoclassic poet, to the release of satire (valuable to himself as well as society), though his dissatisfactions were certainly as great. His liberal and romantic humanitarianism stood in the way; and if he was able to shed it, or more often only to pretend to do so, he quickly encountered his next and more fundamental embarrassment: the great neoclassic satirists had been already there before him. "When a great poet has lived," said Eliot, "certain things have been done once for all, and cannot be achieved again."

True, there was a price, inherited from the half-century between the death of Pope and 1790. In the self-regrounding forced by that question of what was still open to the poet, one of the by-products was a deliberate effort to exploit the uses of poetry for what was called the "agreeable," the uses of poetry (not yet stolen from it by prose) for comfort and consolation. Much of the popular idiom of poetry, from 1750 to World War I, even later, is in this vein – immediately open to comprehension and yet emotionally specialized. (It is on this especially that the antiromantic reaction of the twentieth century concentrated its attack, sometimes with the thought that all you had to do, in establishing your own difference, was to turn things upside down.) Here at least, it was felt, wide acceptability was still left in one way that no other medium seemed able to threaten or to exploit half so well. The result was the sentimental (elegiac, meditative, reflective, or the merely pretty). This was not to be scorned. It had its values. Through it a ladder was available to the reading public as there would not be if what Santayana calls "penitent" art had its way. For those who find no rungs to mount begin to turn elsewhere, and the artist can be left in proud isolation, alone in the barnloft with the drying hay. Yet there were also limitations. The rise up the ladder often led to the nearest thing to an ideological and emotional prison that the greater Romantics faced: the whole concept of the "beautiful." But the struggle to broaden a ruling concept can have its advantages, if only through challenge, and for that purpose there have been some less fruitful than the "beautiful."

But granted all this, nothing thus far mentioned much distinguishes the romantic circumstance proper (after 1780 or 1790) from the latter half of the eighteenth century generally – from the poetry of what Northrop Frye calls "The Age of Sensibility." For it was in the generation before 1790 that poetry found the popular idiom with which it was to continue for at least another century, and it was also already beginning to explore new subject matters and employ a greater particularity of treatment. If we try to account for the sudden romantic success in the 1790's and the thirty years following, is there anything more to be cited than merely the convergence of several elements into an interaction which became self-accelerating, or, as a still more helpless plea, the accident of genius? Obviously there is.

For one thing, there is what we can only call a profound opening up for literary treatment of the "inner" life of the individual. In exploiting this the Romantics relied on at least a hundred years of British empirical psychology. The theme was not taken up without some reluctance. As Wordsworth says at the start of *The Prelude,* he would have preferred to write an epic, romance, or long philosophical poem, and he refused to publish *The Prelude* until he could also show a long work of a more traditional kind. The critical remarks of Keats in his letters, where we see him casting about for his own direction, express the same uneasiness: this poetry of the inner life could forfeit objectivity and range. But at the same time, there was a sense of both its originality and its profound importance. For this poetry, as it "martyrs itself," in Keats's phrase, "to the human heart," not only comes closer to some modes of "truth." It also conveys a new sense of the adventure and possible joy of living. The feeling of this was so strong that Wordsworth, in the Prospectus to *The Excursion,* proclaims that the "Mind of Man" is "My haunt, and the main region of my song," and goes on to voice his "high argument," how the mind can through its own creativity and love make a paradise of common things. The appeal of the subjective theme was powerful enough to deflect Keats from his admiration of the great "objective" genres of the past, making him wonder whether Wordsworth was not "deeper than Milton . . . [Milton] did not think into the human heart, as Wordsworth has done." And in the first of the great odes, "To Psyche," he commits himself to building a temple to this "latest-born" promise for art – the "untrodden region of the mind."

But if the Romantics opened up the subjective world, they were able to do so as greatly as they did, and ultimately with profound and wide appeal, because they refused to view it as an end in itself. They clung at the same time to the advice of their mentors that art can renew itself most fertilely through the inexhaustibility of nature itself. More important for the confidence of the poet than the opportunities of turning to the inner life per se was the recapture of belief in the reality — or at least strong probability — of a unity of being, and, still more important, the corollary and not unreasonable belief that imaginative art is, in its highest function, a means of touching and sharing in it: a belief in, or aspiration toward, a unity of being in which all the usual distinctions — objective and subjective, man and nature, intellect and feeling, conscious and unconscious — were, as René Wellek says, seen as only aspects or modes of the whole. To follow the development of this aspiration seems to me the most rewarding single episode in the history of ideas since the Renaissance. But we cannot linger on it here, least of all on the fascinating differences between one country and another. (In Germany, which lacked a long national tradition in literature, this ideal pervaded every aspect of thought. In England, meanwhile, the poet was more preoccupied with the classical or Renaissance-English past. In France, where the national tradition was so closely interwoven with the neoclassic, the "romantic" was at first primarily a rebellion against or a questioning of the central classical inheritance of France.)

Superficially it could be said that two things simultaneously converge: the "protest on behalf of the *organic* view of nature" that Whitehead described as the essence of Romanticism, and also the century-long development, by British empirical psychology, of the theory of the imagination. But the first really followed from and through the second. For the concept of "organicism" is as old as the history of philosophy and perpetually ready to flower again into active premise or ideal, provided only that we have some confidence that the evolving process of nature is something we can to some degree understand and share — some confidence that the self-defensive cautions and timidities of the mind before the unknown are not inevitable, are not ordained in the eternal scheme of things. If eighteenth-century empiricism opened a Pandora's box of more drastic forms of reductionism than ever before (materialistic, psychological, or merely skeptical), it also—with the strength and freedom that pioneers have to resist slavery to method—turned against its own theoretical militance and broadened, on empirical grounds, its conception of what empiricism (or the use of experience) can mean. The result was a concept of mind entirely "open": the realization that we can, through sympathetic identification, grasp things in their living process and can sense their qualities, not as separate entities, but as an organic part of the concrete totality from which—but only because of our own myopia—we ourselves needlessly isolate them. The spectrum of interpretation could range from the concept of imagination as inspired common sense (as in Hazlitt's essay "On Genius and Common-Sense") to the concept of imagination as the unified grasp of concreteness fulfilling or unfolding the transcendental through living process, or even as direct visionary insight into the essence of things (in which case, as in Blake, the imagination is radically creative and in its way a copartner with the divine in the unfolding drama of creation.) But at any point along the spectrum imagination was conceived as *noetic*, as an indispensable means for the apprehension of truth. And it followed that art, and especially poetry as potentially the most open and articulate of the arts, was also creatively *noetic*. Accordingly, the arts had the highest possible justification. In short, a new life was given, whatever the difference in vocabulary, to the old classical conviction of the formative or educative power of art; and not merely because art can reveal, suggest, or convey truth but because—as it reaches through symbols and varieties of expression to the "whole man," as Coleridge said—it also reawakens and intensifies the "germinal powers of growth and development" in the reader or audience. And whether or not you took the high transcendental road yourself, there was the confidence that at least an adjoining field remained open for the drama of what Keats called the "greeting of the spirit" and its object — for the drama or debate of the heart's aspiration before and with the mystery of reality (the central concern of the odes as it is of *Lamia* and the *Fall of Hyperion*). And if this confidence seems to subside by the middle of the nineteenth century — for example, when we come to the Victorians in England or their counterparts in other countries — it is not because they, or we ourselves a century later, really disapprove of the premises or aspiration. In fact as humanists we have since continued to repeat those very premises, even though we prefer to use another, tamer vocabulary or to cite earlier sources or authorities than the romantic if and when we can discover them.

—9—

And yet when we put all these things together, we do not get the full answer to our question: why the Romantics — these children of the eighteenth century — were able to do what they did despite the apparent odds against them. Nor do we get closer by merely adding other considerations of the same kind — for our list could be extended.* What is still missing is the boldness of spirit that seizes upon opportunities and creates new ones. In that long

* E.g., the French Revolution and the challenges of social change — though our own century has had comparable experiences — or, to cite something radically different, the whole modern conception of the evolution and change of genres themselves — so easy to talk about theoretically, so difficult to insinuate into the habitual responses of those whose task is to create or perform rather than to reflect and advise. For the poet, if he is worth his salt, still remembers *Lear*, and the painter remembers Michelangelo. Our modern sense that genres are not forever stratified as God-given has, seeping into us slowly (against immense inner opposition, including idealistic opposition — with all the possible rigidities as well as advantages of idealism), done something to free the artist. But by itself, unaided by the example of more recent models of another kind from

self-debate during which the eighteenth century seemed to descend theoretically to the belief that so little might still be left for the arts, it also found bedrock. It came to this through its own honesty and essentialism – its ability to cling to essential fact while also keeping hold of essential ideal. The latter – the creative and formative essentialism of ideal – is shown by the fact that throughout the middle and later eighteenth century it rarely occurred to anyone to question the ideal of greatness. The artist as an individual might feel intimidated, even crushed. But the men of that century, and even more the youth of the next generation whom they produced and taught, were haunted by the vision of greatness: "Moral education," said Whitehead – a fundamental education of the whole self into action or being – "is impossible apart from the habitual vision of greatness. If we are not great, it does not matter what we do or what is the issue. Now the sense of greatness is an immediate intuition and not the conclusion of an argument . . . The sense of greatness is the groundwork of morals" – of what one really does and *is*. It is for this reason, more than any other, that the famous work from the first century, Longinus' *On the Sublime*, had, at least since the 1730's, become so central as an authoritative support – at once precept and example (he is "himself the great Sublime he draws," said Pope) – speaking to us from the distant past. This was its primary theme. (The theoretical concept of the "sublime" itself, whether taken simply as "loftiness of spirit," to use Longinus' own phrase, or with all the alternative phrases and nuances this per-

which one can take heart, it can still leave him deeply divided in his sense of what is left him. Perhaps its help has been largely "palliative rather than radical" – what Johnson says is our only hope for most human ills. In any case I do not believe that the liberating influence of the critical theory of the evolution of genres per se had much direct effect on the poet himself (or probably the artist generally) till later in the nineteenth century, and then largely because of the example of romantic models.

mitted, is not what we are speaking about at the moment – though it is at least as relevant to Romanticism as anything else that we ran through in our list. If the concept of the "sublime" enters directly into what are now saying, it is in its more literal sense: a release of what is "below the threshold" of consciousness for fulfillment in and through the great.)

The essential message of Longinus is that, in and through the personal rediscovery of the great, we find that we need not be the passive victims of what we deterministically call "circumstances" (social, cultural, or reductively psychological-personal), but that by linking ourselves through what Keats calls an "immortal free-masonry" with the great we can become freer – freer to be ourselves, to be what we most want and value; and that by caring for the kinds of things that they did we are not only "imitating" them, in the best and most fruitful sense of the word, but also "joining them." Longinus' *On the Sublime* was written during the same century in which Velleius Paterculus wrote the brilliant diagnosis that David Hume resurrected in the 1740's, which then became so alive as a way of understanding what was happening – what would inevitably happen given "the nature and constitution of things" (that phrase of Burke's that is so weighted with what we most value in the eighteenth century – its recognition of fact without the surrender of ideal). Like Velleius Paterculus, Longinus speaks of the condition of the arts in his time, a "later" time: pedestrian imitation or "clever and skillful" uses of the mere medium of art; the inevitable craze for novelty of expression, and the fatigues of the spirit that may crave it.

But always available to man, if he hopes to rise above "cultural declines" and fatigues from whatever cause – or to rise above anything else that threatens to imprison or deflect him personally – is the companionship, the support to the heart and spirit, of a direct and frank turning to the great. The "immortal free-masonry" is forever open to the questing spirit — the spirit that really wishes to "greet." I return to our plea for a reconsideration of the uses of biography — for what Johnson called its principal value — "what comes near to ourselves, what can be put to use." For here alone we see concretely the drama of all we have been saying and the human context within which it works. And it is only within this directly and individually human context that we come close to what I am trying to suggest — noting how time after time, whatever the sinking of spirit, whatever the incentives to inner rebellion, the vision of greatness can operate suddenly as a release as well as an incentive to the creative initiative of the spirit. For we become so reductive when we pluck examples out of their context. How little we appreciate if all we do is to cite quickly such instances as Wordsworth identifying with Milton, Shelley with any number of writers from Aeschylus to Plato to Dante, Byron with Pope and the bold mockery of some of the Renaissance Italian poets, Blake with the Biblical prophets, Keats with Spenser, Milton, and, above all, Shakespeare. One nuance after another could suggest itself after everything we say, including the personal rediscovery, by these writers, of the use of identification with the great in the past for confidence and security, as well as to gain strength in one's antagonism to what is least valued in the present. This is indeed a valuable point. (It was an example of Coleridge's nakedness and vulnerable self-doubt that he alone among the major poets — despite, perhaps because of, his extremely open and dependent nature — seemed unable to do this with any of the greater poets of the past, but could adopt only the role of explainer, admirer, and usher, which was of immense value for criticism if not for his own poetic creativity.) We could also turn to the romantic, generally modern discovery of a further creative use of the past, namely, the active debate or dialogue within the human psyche of the past with the present. This would subsume as one element the struggle of the mind and heart with the welter and fixations of nostalgia. But, more broadly conceived, it involves every attempt to weigh the past against the present and strike the balance of loss and gain. From the romantic period to now this has provided not only a constant theme but a profusion of forms as well — for example, the juxtaposition of images of past and present, as in *The Waste Land,* or the drama in major lyrics of what David Perkins has called "symbolic debate." (An example would be the interplay of the heart's aspirations, embodied in a symbol, with the actual in Keats's "Ode on a Grecian Urn.") Or we could go on to say that cooperating, and at last becoming fruitful for this very reason, was the growing realization of what Coleridge called an "*acknowledged* difference" — a real division between the present and the past. For you could not really be like Milton anyway, said Keats (and he earned the right to say this as no other poet has ever earned it, writing the greatest Miltonic blank verse since Milton, not only with unrivaled technical dexterity but with a far larger commitment that can only be called love): Milton's poetry embodied — in its whole style or expression as well as its high aspiration — an immense loftiness of spirit, but, Keats felt, it depended on particular premises or "resting-places" in the "intellectual world" to which one could no longer return. The loftiness of spirit could still reach out to us, perhaps even more so because we were now standing on a different ground. Perhaps only so could the readiness to turn to the past become truly active and liberating without also becoming intimidating. There was indeed an "acknowledged difference." And when difference is accepted as a fact, then every move toward unity and agreement, as

Coleridge says, is a demonstrable step upward – but only, of course, if there is the animating, creative desire to live and share in the same company. It is of this that we are speaking.

—10—

In everything we have mentioned that may have permitted or encouraged the next great movement in the arts (the modern movement generally, of which Romanticism is the first stage), we found ourselves returning to the heart of the eighteenth century. So, even more, with what we have just now said. Perhaps the greatest lesson the century learned from its long, scrupulous, and imaginatively thoughtful comparison of its own experience with the larger past was the value of boldness; not the *soi-disant* boldness of negativism, of grudgingly withholding assent as we seek to establish our identities, prate of our integrity, or reach into our pockets for our mite of "originality." None of us, as Goethe said, is really very "original" anyway; one gets most of what he attains in his short life from others. The boldness desired involves directly facing up to what we admire and then trying to be like it (the old Greek ideal of education, of *paideia*, of trying to be like the excellence, or *arete*, that we have come to admire – whatever our self-defensive protests). It is like that habit of Keats of beginning each large new effort by rereading *Lear* and keeping always close at hand the engraving of Shakespeare that he found in the lodging house in the Isle of Wight when he went off to begin *Endymion*. In a sense, what this typifies was true of them all: true at least of the greatest artists (Wordsworth, looking constantly back as he did to Milton; Beethoven, who in his last days kept rereading the scores of Handel; Goethe, who returned to the Greeks or to Shakespeare). In effect, they ended – at their best – in defying the taboo that they inherited and that so many of their contemporaries were strengthening.

To reduce that taboo to size, to get ourselves out of this self-created prison, to heal or overcome this needless self-division, has been the greatest single problem for modern art. And in saying this, we are also speaking of something even larger – the freedom of man (that freedom so indispensable to achievement) to follow openly and directly what he most values: what he has been taught to value, what he secretly or openly wishes he had done or could do.

For the brute fact remains that in no other aspect of life (only in the arts during the last two centuries, and hardly ever in the arts before then to any serious degree) do you have a situation where the whole procedure of what to do with your life, your vocation, your craft – the whole process of learning and achievement – has at times seemed about to be crazily split down the middle by two opposing demands. On the one hand, we have the natural human response to great examples that, from childhood up, are viewed as prototypes (in statecraft, science, religion, or anything else – including even the hero worship and desire for emulation in gangsters). In no other case do you have this natural response of the human heart and mind exercised through education, encouraged, and gradually absorbed into the conscience and bloodstream – and then have suddenly blocking it a *second* injunction: the injunction that you are forbidden to be very closely like these examples. In no other case are you enjoined to admire and at the same time to try, at all costs, *not* to follow closely what you admire, not merely in detail but in overall procedure, in general object, in any of the broader conventions of mode, vocabulary, or idiom. Yet here, in the arts, this split is widening, and not only widening but being argued with helpless militancy on each side.

The essence of neurosis is conflict. When we face obviously conflicting demands, when the pressures (or what we imagine the pressures to be) are ones that enjoin us to move in two different – in fact, two opposing – directions at once, what do we do then? I think of the fable of the donkey that starved when he was confronted, on each side, with two equally distant bales of hay. The arts stutter, stagger, pull back into paralysis and indecision before such a conflict of demand.

In this dilemma the arts mirror the greatest single cultural problem we face, assuming that we physically survive: that is, how to use a heritage, when we know and admire so much about it, how to grow by means of it, how to acquire our own "identities," how to be ourselves. And as we now try to reground our thinking, in turning back again to the essential to discover what next to do (to be, to hope for), we have the companionship, if we choose to avail ourselves of it, of the period that first encountered what we ourselves face now: which took for granted so much that we may now be saying ourselves, which indeed anticipated it – even laid the foundations for it – and yet was self-corrective because of its honesty, because of its freedom from any fear of facing either fact or ideal. They were already there before us. In the experience of the eighteenth century we have exemplified – if we choose to look at it with a "greeting of the spirit" – what the old epigram said of Plato (something I have often thought applies to Johnson): that, in whatever direction you happened to be going, you met him on his way back.

Index

Addison, Joseph, 39
Aeschylus, 130
Ages of poetry, *see* Golden Age
Alexander the Great, 70
Alison, Archibald, on emulation and pursuit of innovation, 83–84, 97–98
Ancients and Moderns, quarrel of, 23–25
Apelles, 70
Aristides the Just, 84
Aristotle, 112; on art as imitation, 18; on novelty, 106

Bach, J. S., 8, 32
Bacon, Francis, 62, 65; on modern theater, 69
Beethoven, L. van, 8, 13, 33, 120, 132
Berkeley, George, 120
Biography, literary: avoidance of central problem for writers, 7–10, 115–116; uses of, 116, 130
Blackmore, Sir Richard, 42–43, 110
Blackwell, Thomas, 99; on Homer and impossibility of epic now, 49–50
Blair, Hugh, 99; poetry more vigorous in earlier periods, 62
Blake, William, 33, 118, 130; on independence from past, 89–90
Bloom, Harold, ix
Boileau, Nicolas, 21, 39; asks where modern Virgil is, 40
Boswell, James, 45, 68, 84
Brown, John, on separation and decline of arts, 50–51, 88
Burke, Edmund, 13, 45, 84, 90, 105, 106
Burns, Robert, 47, 90
Burton, Robert, 39
Bush, Douglas, ix
Byron, George Gordon, Lord, 118, 119, 130; on fickleness in taste, 84

Cervantes, Miguel de, 38
Chaucer, Geoffrey, 44
Chesterfield, Earl of, as patron of "unspoiled geniuses," 47
Clare, John, 47
Classical: effect of ideals on neoclassic, 21–22; 34–45; ideal of *arete*, 57, 132. *See also* Ancients and Moderns, Golden Age, Primitivism
Coleridge, S. T.: modesty before past, 91; intimidating ideal of poetry, 109–110; other references, vii, x, 9, 33, 116, 120, 126
Collins, William, and idea of decline, 44–45
Condillac, E. B. de, on progress in all things but art, 46
Congreve, William, Dryden's lines to, 26, 39
Constable, John, on earlier art's recourse to nature, 111
Corot, J. B. C., 73
Correctness, as "one way left of excelling," 31. *See also* Decorum
Cowley, Abraham, 35
Cowper, William, 119
Crabbe, George, 119
Critic, lesser burden of past upon, 7–8. *See also* Criticism, Neoclassicism, Romanticism
Criticism: inhibitions created by, 54–57, 87, 97–98; demand for novelty, 98–103
Cromwell, Oliver, 16

Dante Alighieri, 3, 63, 75, 130; Landor on, 74
Decline, in the arts: concepts of, viii, 9–11, 26–27; contrast with cumulative sciences, 40, 44, 46–54, 61–65; regarded as product of social conditions, 49–50, of specialism in arts, 50–51, of changes in language, 51–52, of other factors, 53–56; and emulation, *see* Emulation
Decorum, neoclassic concept of, 18–20
De Quincey, Thomas, on literature of knowledge and power, 8
Demosthenes, 70
Dickens, Charles, 3, 8, 119
Drama, poetic: effect of Shakes-

peare on, 5–6; Dryden on new modes of, 25–26; anxieties about decline in, 44, 61–62, 76–79; the novel compared with, 103; problem for Romantics, 112–113
Dryden, John: on rhyme in tragedy as unexploited mode, 25; concept of "Second Temple," 26–27; first great poet to assume past creates need for difference, 31; on Shakespeare, 44; other references, 4, 16, 32, 33, 39, 45, 106, 122
Duck, Stephen, 47
Duff, William, 99; on original genius in earlier societies, 50

Eighteenth century: pivotal period, vii, 12–13; artificial division between romantic and, viii–ix, 33, 127; first to face burden of past, 12–13; perfects second, creates third major modern movement, 33, 106; use of classical, 34–39; self-debate on neoclassicism, 42–57; cult of originality, 47, 104–107; creative value of criticism in, 56–57; gains since Renaissance, 84–85
Elegance, as neoclassic ideal, 41
Eliot, T. S.: on poets exhausting chances for successors, 4, 122; other references, 15, 22, 131
Emerson, R. W.: on Milton and Shakespeare, 61–62, 97; on the familiar, 117
Emulation, and rise and decline of arts, 80–84. *See also* Hume, David
Epic: considered no longer possible, 49–50; decline regretted, 61–62; Schlegel on, 71; as overrated, 74–75; as more limited genre than drama, 77–79; Coleridge on requirements for, 109

Ferguson, Adam, on primitive language, 52
Fielding, Henry, 38
Frye, Northrop, ix, 73, 123; on modal grandfather, 22
Fuseli, Henry, ix, 90

Genius, original: greater in earlier periods, 54, 61–65; and emulation, *see* Hume, David. *See also* Originality
Gerard, Alexander, 83, 99
Gibbon, Edward, 49, 90; ridicules Warton on Greeks, 70
Gildon, Charles, 24
Goethe, J. W. von: on difficulties of English poet following Shakespeare, 5–6; on effects of criticism, 87; on intimidation by the past, 96; on originality and turning to nature, 111–112, 117, 132; other references, 3, 33, 84, 90, 106, 118
Golden Age: in arts, primitivistic considerations and, 48–53; as "second" (post-"iron") period in a culture, 53–54, 63–65, 67; use of "whole mind" in, 62; sentimentalization of, 67–71
Goldsmith, Oliver, 9; and idea of decline, 45, 55, 62, 84
Granville, George (Lord Lansdowne), 20
Guthrie, William, 24

Handel, G. F., 32, 42, 132
Hanmer, Sir Thomas, 44
Hazlitt, William, 16, 114, 118, 121; on decline of poetic drama, 112–113; "On Genius and Common-Sense," 126; "Why the Arts Are Not Progressive," 108
Hegel, G. W. F., 14, 15, 82
Herod, and Third Temple, 27
Homer: Pope on, 44; Blackwell on, 49; other references, 3, 38, 41, 56, 63, 69, 71, 72, 74, 75, 77, 89
Hugo, Victor, 120
Hume, David, 13, 104, 117; on place of emulation in rise and decline of arts, 80–84, 86, 88, 95, 99, 103, 129
Hurd, Richard: on "golden age" of Elizabeth, 54; on anxiety for

novelty and dread of imitation, 86
Imitation: neoclassic uses of, 37–38; fear of, 86
Inner life, romantic opening of, for literature, 123–125
Invention, *see* Originality

James, William, 13
Jeffrey, Francis, 16, 73; on gap between popular and critical taste, 99–103; on hope for novel, 103
Johnson, Samuel: on inhibiting ideas, viii; on danger of following great writers, 3; on tendency to censure rather than praise, 24; on elegance, 41; on poetry of own time, 45, 84–85; dislike of idea of decline, 61, 77–78; on nostalgia, 67–68; on critical fastidiousness, 75; on superstitious reverence of dead, 77; on recourse to nature, 78, 111; on imitation, 85; on novelty and originality, 85–86, 106; on Shakespeare, 86; on value of common reader, 98; on dogma of unities, 118; other references, vii, 20, 43, 84, 89, 90, 102, 121, 128, 134
Jonson, Ben, 14

Kaiser, Walter, ix
Kames, Lord, 99; on emulation, 83
Kant, Immanuel, 33
Keats, John: sense of burden of past, 5; on moderns vs. Elizabethans, 61, 108; on the long poem, 76; on epic, 77; dramatic character of lyrics, 78–79, 127, 131; on Milton, 102, 124, 131; struggle with conflicting ideals, 108; on poetry of inner life, 124; other references, vii, x, 9, 114, 118, 119, 130
Koestler, Arthur, on snobbery, 72

La Bruyère, Jean de, 39
Lamb, Charles, 109
Landor, W. S.: on decline, 64; on Homer and Dante, 74
Language, development from concrete to abstract, 51–52, 64
Lessing, G. E., 84, 90
Levin, Harry, ix
Lewes, G. H., 74
Locke, John, 5, 117
Longfellow, H. W., 119
Longinus, 56; belief in confidence and spirit as contagious, 77n; message of, and its effect, 128–132 *passim*
Lyric, romantic bias toward, 113–115. *See also* Pure poetry
Lyttelton, Lord, Johnson on, 85

Macaulay, T. B., Lord, on decline of poetry as inevitable, 64
Malskat, Lothar, forgeries by, 72–73
Mann, Thomas, 8; *Dr. Faustus* and modern artist, 10–11, 98
Marie Antoinette, 47
Michelangelo, 8, 45, 83, 89
Milton, John: popularity in 18th century, 22, 69–70; as example to poets, 77n; and Wordsworth, 124, 132; other references, 3, 17, 37, 42, 43, 61, 63, 64, 74, 75, 87, 88, 89, 102, 129, 130, 131
Monboddo, Lord, 99
Moore, Thomas, 119
Moritz, K. P., 22, 70, 87
Mozart, W. A., 13
Music: Mann's *Dr. Faustus* and, 10–11; contrast with literature in 18th century, 31–32

Neoclassicism, in England: reasons for its occurrence, 14–27; retrenchment, 31–33; basic dilemma, 34–45; reconsideration of, 45–48
Newton, Sir Isaac, 5, 18, 25, 104; decline in study of mathematics after, 83
Nietzsche, Friedrich, 51
Nostalgia, treacheries of historical, 67–75
Novel: and anti-romance, 38; still open as form in 1800, 97; likely

to face same problems as poetry, 103
Novelty: argued by neoclassic as unnecessary, 39–40; dangers in pursuing per se, 81, 85–86; awakens attention, 106. *See also* Golden Age, Nostalgia, Originality

Organic, romantic concept of nature as, 125–127
Originality: despaired of by neoclassic, 36, 39–45; earlier periods excel in, 48–50; possibility of, when nature directly faced, 77–78, 85–86, 111; problem of, 95–103; becomes conscious ideal, even fetish, 104–107; and Longinian identification with great, 128–134
Ortega y Gasset, José: on comparisons with past, 71; on sophisticated vs. popular art, 120–121

Pater, Walter, 85
Peacock, T. L., "Four Ages of Poetry," 63
Pericles, 70
Perkins, David, ix–x; on effect of ideal of sincerity, 107; on modern poetry of symbolic debate, 131
Phidias, 70
Plato, 70, 130, 134
Pliny, on burden of past on statesmen, 3
Plotz, Judith, ix
Poe, E. A., on "pure" poetry, 74
Pope, Alexander: on correctness as only way left of excelling, 31; on invention, 36; on the "correctly cold," 39; his success a problem for later poets, 44, 84n, 90; other references, 17, 24–25, 32, 43, 122, 130
Popular, the: split between sophisticated art and, 23, 98–103; and 18th-century idiom, 37; and open idiom of 19th-century poets, 119–122
Priestley, Joseph: on future of poetry, 65, 96; on emulation and arts, 83
Primitivism, and fear of decline in arts, 47–51, 53, 62–65, 67–69, 71
Progress, *see* Decline
Pure poetry, concept of, 74–76, 113

Raphael, 83, 96
Refinement, neoclassic ideal of, 39, 42–44, 81, 84
Rembrandt van Rijn, 8, 73
Renaissance: changes in arts since, 4, 10; inventive originality, 20; renewed appreciation of, 43–45; emulation of Greece, 80–81. *See also* Milton, Originality, Shakespeare
Reynolds, Sir Joshua, 84, 90, 118; on Johnson, ix, 68; on Michelangelo, 45
Robinson, Crabb, 74
Robinson, E. A., 50
Romanticism: child of 18th century, viii–ix, 33, 127; transition to, vs. shift to neoclassicism, 17; ideal of Elizabethan and baroque drama, 76–77; initiates third great movement in arts and thought, 95–134 *passim*; characteristics of, 115–127; popular nature of, 119–122; opens inner life, 123–124; salutary effect of ideal of sublime on, 127–133
Rousseau, J. J., 7
Rymer, Thomas, 16

Sainte-Beuve, C. A., on late-comers in literature, 32
Santayana, George, 56; on "penitent" art, 115, 123
Scheffer, J. D., on decline, 48n
Schiller, J. C. F. von, 33, 84, 90; "On Naive and Sentimental Poetry," 71–72
Schlegel, Friedrich von: on epic, 71, 75; on modern opportunities, 79
Science, contrast with arts, 7, 11, 40, 46, 87
Scott, Sir Walter, 118; attempt at popular, 100, 102

Self-consciousness: greatest problem of modern art, 3–4; increased by criticism, 54–57, 87, 97–99. *See also* Popular, the
Shaftesbury, Earl of, 5
Shakespeare, William: Goethe on effect on later writers, 5–6; Dryden on, 44; inhibiting effect of, 79–80; Johnson on, 86; Keats's ideal of, 132; other references, 3, 17, 32, 43, 61, 62, 63, 64, 69, 71, 73, 75, 87, 89, 109, 116, 130
Shelley, P. B., 130
Sidney, Sir Philip, 14
Sincerity, as complicating ideal, 107
Smith, Adam, 99; on progressive abstraction of language, 52
Sophisticated art, *see* Popular, the
Sophocles, 3, 89
Southey, Robert, 110
Specialism, progressive, in arts and language, 50–51, 62
Spender, Stephen, on modern writer, 6–7
Spengler, Oswald, 9, 82
Spenser, Edmund, 130
Steele, Sir Richard, 40
Steiner, George, on origins of Romanticism, 76–77
Sublime, *see* Longinus
Swift, Jonathan, on Ancients and Moderns, 23–24, 38

Temple, Sir William, 16, 46, 55
Tennyson, Alfred, Lord, 21
Thomson, James, 18
Tillotson, Geoffrey, ix
Titian, 83
Tragedy, *see* Drama
Trilling, Lionel, on modern literature, 55, 104

Velleius Paterculus, on emulation and rise and decline in arts, 82–83, 129
Vico, G. B., 9
Virgil, 40–41, 69, 74, 77
Voltaire, 84, 106; on decline as inevitable in arts, 46; on quest for novelty as doomed, 86

Wagner, Richard, 120
Walsh, William, advises Pope on correctness as ideal, 31
Warton, Joseph, 55; idealization of past, 68, 70
Warton, Thomas, on "golden age" of Elizabeth, 54, 87
Wasserman, Earl, ix
Watteau, J. A., 73
Wellek, René, 125
Whitehead, A. N., x, 57, 118; on Romanticism and organicism, 125; on moral education and ideal of greatness, 128
Wilson, John, 99; on modern tendency toward lyric, 113
Wordsworth, William, 33, 49, 114, 117, 129, 132; on comparing past with present, 70–71; relative self-confidence of, 108–109; takes human mind as subject, 124

Yeats, W. B., 23; on loss of range in poetry, 62
Young, Edward, on intimidation by past writers, 55–56, 71, 85